T0149415

The author has written a number of other non-fiction books including:

A Guide to Running Your first Marathon

For details about this and other books go to:

www.douglimbrick.com
Comments can be sent to: info@douglimbrick.com

RUNNING
THE **MARATHON** WITH
CANCER

A story about life, love, running,
friendships, personal growth, self discovery
& surviving colorectal cancer

Doug Limbrick

BALBOA.
PRESS

A DIVISION OF HAY HOUSE

Balboa Press books may be ordered through booksellers or by contacting:

Balboa Press
A Division of Hay House
1663 Liberty Drive
Bloomington, IN 47403
www.balboapress.com.au
1 (877) 407-4847

Print information available on the last page.

ISBN: 978-1-5043-0784-0 (sc)
ISBN: 978-1-5043-0783-3 (e)

Balboa Press rev. date: 05/23/2017

This book is dedicated to my wife, Penny, family and friends
who provided an enormous amount of love and care
during my illness and recovery,
including those who I ran with when times were good
and who continued to 'run' with me when times were difficult.

The unexamined life is not worth living.

Socrates

Acknowledgements

While I have previously written other books this is my first attempt at writing a story about myself. I would thus like to thank my family and friends for the encouragement they provided during the writing of this book. A special thanks to those who read some early drafts and offered comments and suggestions, which I trust I have faithfully incorporated. I am grateful for the assistance and suggestions provided by my editor Dr Pam Faulks (Clarity Proofreading & Editing). A big thanks to Jeremy Limbrick for graphics assistance and suggestions particularly for the cover design.

Contents

List of Illustrations

Introduction

Although you may not always be able to avoid difficult situations, you can modify the extent to which you suffer by how you choose to respond to the situation.

Dalai Lama

I am a cancer survivor and I am a runner.

I have been a runner for over 30 years. It all started because I decided that I needed to do something about my lack of fitness. After a slow beginning and what seemed like a long period of pain (because of my very poor level of fitness) I seemed to cross over a threshold – the degree of difficulty involved in running finally decreased. I had managed to persist with the running long enough to gain a small level of fitness. And after a few more weeks I started to look forward to my running; I found other lunchtime runners and enjoyed their company and encouragement. I entered a few events and was encouraged to join a club. By this time I was running most days and had extended the distance from the initial 1 or 2 kilometre struggle around the streets near my home to 8 to 10 kilometres over a range of terrain.

I found that I was by now part of a large running community of all ages and abilities. I discovered that the benefits that I derived from running were not just related to physical fitness but also mental fitness. The running gave me more confidence in my abilities and equipped me to handle busy and stressful work situations more easily and competently. My daily run had become extremely important to my wellbeing. I had fallen in love with running.

Hence this story is not just about surviving cancer; it's also a story about running. It's a story about the part running has played in my life and in my ability to deal with cancer treatment – to survive, to rehabilitate myself, to appreciate health and to move on with normal life. Over the years running has helped me discover some things about myself, and I found that during my time with cancer running helped me to discover even more. And through the running community I met some wonderful friends that are also part of this story.

Soon after my first surgery for my cancer, while still in hospital, I started to make some fairly rough notes about what was happening to me. At first these notes were about events and were a distraction from treatment, but as time went on I started to incorporate comments about my observations and gradually I moved to recording my feelings. My initial intention was to keep writing about having cancer – about my treatment and my experiences as a type of therapy for myself. However, when my situation changed dramatically and I had a long period in hospital, including two weeks in the Intensive Care Unit (ICU), I had lots of time to think and to reassess my priorities in life. My writing style and purpose changed from rough notes into something more thoughtful and I started to develop a story about a journey. One night while lying awake in the ICU I imagined writing a book about having cancer as a way of sharing my experience (and possibly getting through the night). I have held this thought in my mind for some time. However, it took a considerable amount of further thinking about why I had cancer, why I survived and what had I learnt from the experience that convinced me to turn my notes and subsequent thinking into this story.

My aim is to share and inform others about what it's like to have cancer, to be treated, to have many setbacks and to reflect on this in terms of what I have learnt and what life is like after cancer.

Having cancer forced me to face a number of issues, which led to considerable personal growth. This included exploring over and over the question of understanding who I am. The real me. Thus this book is also about my personal journey.

In writing this book I have also had lots of time to think about how important my family and friends were during each stage from diagnosis to recovery. I have learnt much about the importance of friends and the value I need to place on them. Many of my friends, including my running mates, were with me during the highs and lows that were part of the cancer treatment process. They were also very important in my rehabilitation process and my ability to return to running.

The title I chose for this book is of course a play on words. When I was diagnosed with cancer I was already an experienced marathon runner (some of my friends may have said that I was addicted to distance running). My cancer treatment was taking longer and longer, and becoming more complex as time went by, and just like my marathons, the finish line was at times barely visible.

Based on current trends 1 in 12 Australians will develop colorectal cancer before the age of 85. The rate in Australia is high but similar to other developed countries (United States, Canada, New Zealand, Western Europe). My diagnosis prompted many friends and work colleagues to be tested and many were found to have polyps, which can become cancerous. I am pleased they were spared the pain and disruption to life that I underwent. If my story prompts others to be tested I will consider this book to have been an enormous success, and if some of you decide to take up running then I am sure that your life will be enriched by running as mine has been.

I hope that you find my story interesting, informative and thought provoking.

Doug Limbrick

Chapter 1

Fit People Don't Get Cancer

How much happiness is gained, and how much misery escaped, by the frequent and violent agitation of the body.

Dr Samuel Johnson (1709-1784)

We stood together in the shade of the large plane trees – Richard, PK, Adrian and I – slowly munching on some cold and sweet-tasting watermelon. Little was said as we were all somewhat absorbed in our thoughts, contemplating what we had just completed. It was now about 9.30 am and the summer temperature was starting to rise significantly, signalling another hot day. We had been together since 6.30 that morning, running up and down some challenging hills in a national park a few kilometres from the city we live in. Our legs were aching and our bodies were tired after running this challenging 34-kilometre course for some 2 hours 45 minutes. However, despite the aches and pains we were all quietly pleased with our achievement and we all knew that we were now almost ready to run a marathon.

For the past three months we had gathered each Saturday morning to run together, progressively increasing the time and distance. Other runners occasionally joined our group and sometimes one or two mountain bike riders accompanied us. We all felt that this type of training was necessary to be able to run the 42.2 kilometres of the marathon and produce our best performance. The core group of four were a disparate group in ages, abilities and marathon experience: the youngest was 32 and I occupied the senior position being in my 64th year; two members were hoping to improve on their previous marathon performances; and I was training for my 21st marathon.

During these months of training together on this challenging course our friendships also deepened. While we bonded over our common running goal, we also bonded in other ways as we supported each other through the shared experience of pushing our bodies up and down long and steep hills, week after week. During that three-month period each of us had at least one bad day on this demanding course and were 'pulled along' by the support and encouragement of the others in the group. I am sure that similar experiences can occur through other activities, but it certainly takes place through running.

Marathon day came quickly after our last long run together, which we followed with a short tapering period to ensure that our legs would be fresh for the 42.2 kilometres that lay ahead. It was a cool autumn morning when we gathered waiting for the 7 am start. The last minute trips to the toilet were evidence of our pre-start jitters.

Following some last minute words of support and handshakes we lined up with the other runners. After a short wait the gun was fired and we were off on our 42.2-kilometre journey.

Some 3 hours and 20 minutes later I crossed the finish line, hurting and tired but very pleased I had completed my 21st marathon. I finished strongly, passing many runners in the last 10 kilometres, and my time for the event was faster than my time the previous year.

The group was finally all finished and as we hugged one another I felt tears run down my cheeks. Why was I crying and why did I feel so emotional about finishing this marathon? I remember finishing my first marathon and feeling very emotional. In fact I was on a high for over a week and all I could think about was the next one.

Marathon running is, I suspect, like other endurance sports in that it takes you way out of your comfort zone and into an area that requires both physical and mental effort and training. I have run many half marathons and participated in lots of tough mountain and cross-country running events. They all required effort and training but the marathon is different. It takes you to another level where you can fail badly and hit the wall, or where you can achieve your goal and succeed physically and mentally. I recall after several attempts I achieved my goal of running a sub three-hour marathon and how emotional I felt and how that feeling lasted for a number of days. I knew what it was like to feel emotional after completing a marathon; why then was I crying uncontrollably?

The reason was that I had a secret that I had not as yet shared with my running mates. Ten days before the marathon I had been diagnosed with rectal cancer, which I had been told had been growing in my body for some time and I needed to have surgery to remove the cancer as soon as possible. I had made a decision to run the marathon and not to pass on the news of the diagnosis to my running mates until after the event. They didn't know it but they would become part of my journey with cancer.

Ten days before the marathon I had been to hospital for a colonoscopy, which I had assumed, given my excellent state of health and fitness, would reveal no abnormality. Even though I was 63 this was a new experience for me, as I had never had a colonoscopy. The process had involved a special diet two days before the procedure and fasting the day before, accompanied by the consumption of a salty and sickly liquid (designed to clean me out). For the colonoscopy an anaesthetic was administered via an intravenous cannula inserted in the back of the hand. This was followed by a couple of questions from the anaesthetist and from the gastroenterologist and then I remember being aware of the sound of people talking nearby. I had the feeling that I should be asleep waiting for the procedure to start and so I kept my eyes closed and tried to sleep. However the noise persisted and when I looked I was back in the recovery bed. I was soon offered refreshments, which arrived at about the same time as Penny (my wife), who had come to take me home. Penny sat by the bed and talked while I ate (hungry from no food the previous day). Before I had time to finish eating the gastroenterologist arrived and, looking rather formal, proceeded to pull the curtain around the bed. I immediately felt a little uneasy about this situation. He looked at both of us, paused, and then gave us the news that I had rectal cancer.

There was a period of silence, which seemed to last for ages but was in fact only a few seconds long. Penny and I looked at each other in disbelief. I seem to recall shaking my head, and feeling a sensation of numbness, which was I think my immediate way of handling the shock. I was thinking, 'how could someone who was so fit, who didn't smoke, who was extremely healthy, who ate all the right foods, have cancer?' I wanted to explain these facts to the gastroenterologist and get him to reconsider what he had just said. However, the reality of the situation kicked in and so I kept my thoughts to myself. (This kind of irrational thinking would reoccur from time to time.)

While I had never before had a colonoscopy, I had been involved several times in bowel cancer screening tests when I as in my forties. Apart from these tests I had regular health checks, involving an annual blood test and a physical examination by my GP (General Practitioner). During the previous three years I had also had several comprehensive health assessments done by a professional health assessment organisation. These assessments had involved a blood test, a comprehensive examination and a family history and lifestyle assessment. On each occasion I had achieved the best overall score of those in my work group.

It's clear that, despite being fit and having regular health assessments, my cancer could not be detected without having a more thorough testing process, such as a colonoscopy. I have of course asked myself the question many times why had I not had one previously. I believed that I was so fit and healthy that it didn't occur to me that I would ever have a need for further testing. Why then did I decide to have one now?

Following my last comprehensive health assessment I met with my GP and discussed the several pages of the report, a practice that I had developed in the previous two years. In the context of this discussion my doctor suggested that it might be timely for me to have a colonoscopy in order to complete the assessment picture. I was given a list of gastroenterologists but the decision to proceed with a consultation was left to me. Within two weeks I had arranged an appointment and was sitting in the consulting room with the doctor. The gastroenterologist took my history and then gave me a thorough physical examination. He concluded that I was clearly very fit and he could find no trace or indication of a problem. His concluding advice was that the only way to be sure was to have a colonoscopy.

I had never been in hospital, had not required any medical intervention, had not been sick (even with a cold) for the previous 30 years, and so this procedure seemed to me to be a little unnecessary and somewhat invasive. However the gastroenterologist explained that although it would involve inserting a small camera into my large bowel via the rectum, I would be unaware what was occurring, as an anaesthetic would be administered. He also explained that there were risks but that they were very small risks. The risks included perforation of the bowel wall. He also indicated that sometimes polyps are found during a colonoscopy, which are usually a benign growth in the lining of the bowel. They are sometimes attached to the lining by a stalk and can almost always be removed without surgery during a colonoscopy. The reason for removing them is that they can sometimes develop into a cancer. As well as being advised about the restricted diet and fasting in the lead up to the procedure, I was also advised that I would need to prepare by eating and drinking only certain foods two days prior to the procedure and then fasting the day before. I was told that I'd be given a kit containing sachets of powder that I should dissolve in water and drink at particular intervals during the day. This was to ensure that the bowel was as clean as possible for the camera to have the best possible view.

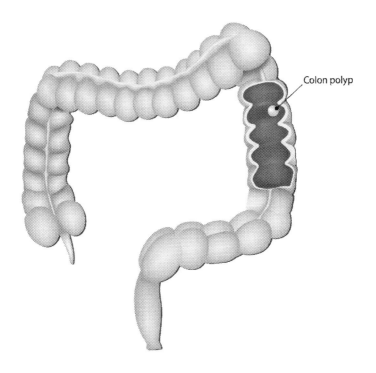

Colon – Showing Polyps

I agreed to proceed with the colonoscopy. In retrospect had I not done so you would probably not be reading this book.

It's interesting that I had none of the usual symptoms of rectal cancer even though the cancer had been present for some time (possibly years). Apparently in the early stages there are usually no symptoms, but then, as the disease progresses – which can take years – symptoms, such as constipation or diarrhoea, weight loss, abdominal pain or tenderness, cramping and fatigue, start to appear. I had none of these symptoms. Even during a thorough physical examination I had no signs of tenderness. I certainly wasn't suffering fatigue as I had just completed three months of hard marathon preparation, and although this rendered me tired at times, I was not fatigued.

The gastroenterologist advised me that the prognosis was good and that I should recover fully after the removal of the cancer. He probably said other things about the possible treatment but I don't remember much about that conversation, as I was preoccupied with the news that I had rectal cancer. I do remember him saying that I may need radiotherapy to shrink the cancer prior to surgery and that he had made an appointment for me to see a surgeon. I left the hospital with many questions buzzing around in my head. What would radiotherapy be like? What would the surgery involve? Would I recover fully? Would I have any permanent difficulties or problems as a result of the treatment?

Colorectal (colon and rectal) cancer, or bowel cancer, is one of the most common cancers. According to Bowel Cancer Australia there are around 15,000 cases diagnosed in Australia each year, but fewer than 40 per cent of these are detected at the early stages of the cancer. Chances of survival are good if the cancer is identified prior to spreading beyond the bowel, but having been advised that my rectal cancer had been there for some time I was wondering if it might have spread. However I would have to wait a little longer to have this and other questions answered.

We left the hospital and the gastroenterologist clutching a discharge paper with notes on next steps, a referral to a surgeon, a blood test form and forms to have an MRI (magnetic resonance imaging) scan and a CT (computerised tomography) scan. I also had a nice rather graphic colour photograph to take with me of my cancer taken during the colonoscopy.

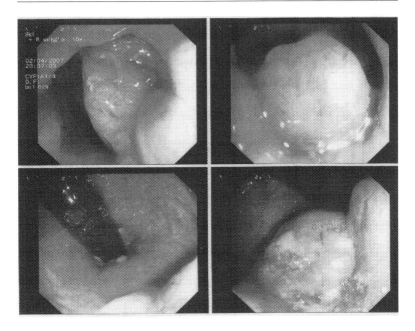

The Photographic Results of my Colonoscopy

It's interesting that one of my recurring thoughts about this diagnosis and the possible consequences was to contemplate what this might mean for my running. Would I still be able to run? Could I still run marathons? Would I still be as competitive in my age group? For the non-runner these thoughts might appear a little bizarre, but running was a significant part of my life, and had been for over 30 years. Every morning my first priority was to go for my daily run. It didn't matter if I was away from home I would still get up early enough to fit a run in to the schedule for the day. I travelled to many places as part of my work and as a result I have run around the streets in many towns and cities including in a number of overseas cities (a great way to see new sights). If I missed my run I felt cheated, particularly from the clarity of mind that came to me through running. I always felt that I didn't perform as well at my job if I missed a morning run. And hence my fears were real.

While I also thought about some of the other possible

consequences of having cancer, the potential impact on my running was ever present. I have been told more than once that I must be mad, that my body would disintegrate, that it was unnatural (we weren't meant to run) and that running is selfish. My experience is, in fact, contrary to all these claims.

My running is very good for my mental health, my body has not disintegrated, it feels natural to me to run (we run as kids and only stop because adults tell us to slow down and walk) and I have made many wonderful friends through running. I have never regretted going for a run, even on those mornings when I was feeling tired, it was minus 3 degrees Celsius outside and it was nice and warm in bed. I would soon warm up and get into a rhythm. The water on my body during a shower always felt better after a run. Soon after I started running regularly I noticed changes to my body – both physically and mentally. When I ran I felt calmer, I could concentrate more easily and for longer periods, I felt more in control of my life and I was much more confident in my ability to cope with whatever I encountered in my job and in my life more broadly. It's interesting to observe the increasing number of studies that are showing the mental health benefits that are derived from running and how it is being recommended for people with significant anxiety, depression and other mental health problems. And because of my running I was lean and healthy looking. Running had become a way of life for me. How would I cope if I couldn't run?

Penny was also in shock following my diagnosis and, like me, she had many questions. The night of the diagnosis we decided to go to a restaurant for dinner. It was a belated wedding anniversary celebration and quickly became a celebration of life. We both decided that this cancer would only present a temporary setback, that I would recover fully, that we would only need to postpone our travel plans and that I would certainly be back to running again after my treatment. We were to have many such discussions over the ensuing months.

That night I had difficulty sleeping, which was unusual for me.

I awoke the next morning still in shock, with a sense of disbelief that I had rectal cancer and still not fully believing that this was actually happening to me. I now needed to prepare for some tests and a meeting with a surgeon the following week.

Chapter 2

What Now?

Positive thinkers think about what's possible. In concentrating on the possibilities, they make things happen.

Follow Your Heart. Andrew Matthews

In preparation for my meeting with the surgeon I was required to have a blood test, an MRI scan (magnetic resonance imaging) and a CT scan (computerised tomography – also known as a CAT scan). I quickly had the blood test but had to wait a few days to secure an appointment for the MRI and CT scans. The MRI scan was long and noisy. The scanners are gigantic humming electro magnets that spin and excite all the hydrogen nuclei in our bodies. Then it lets them relax and turns this into pictures. Unlike the CT scan and X-ray there is no radiation exposure with the MRI. The CT scan, in comparison to the MRI, was relatively quick and involved an intravenous injection containing ionising radiation. At that time I was not aware that I would have many blood tests and CT scans as part of my treatment and the subsequent follow-up process.

Following the scans I returned to work and during the day I had a phone call from a close radiologist friend, Malcolm, who had access to my scans. He had some good news. The scans indicated that it appeared that the cancer was located in the muscle tissue of the rectum wall and had not escaped through the rectum wall. If this were the case it would simplify treatment. The news about the location of the cancer was good and increased my optimism that I would be fine and that I would return to work after a short period of convalescence.

A week after the diagnosis Penny and I were sitting in the consulting rooms of the surgeon waiting to be called. We sat quietly, both a little nervous. We tried with difficulty to make conversation. My mouth felt dry. We wondered what the surgeon would conclude from the blood test and scan results. What would he propose?

Finally my name was called by the surgeon, who came forward and shook hands. He was tall with some slight signs of grey in his hair, which gave him the appearance of someone still relatively young but mature, and someone we could have confidence in. We had been advised that he was a very competent surgeon. Over the following months I would become very familiar with these consulting rooms and this man.

After some preliminary discussion and some questions about my medical history I was examined. This included a rather vigorous rectal examination, which resulted in some bleeding but was necessary to enable the surgeon to locate and explore the dimensions and position of the cancer (this was a procedure that I unfortunately would become very familiar with). While this was happening (possibly to distract myself from the discomfort) I had some weird thoughts about the removal of the cancer (irrational thoughts again). I visualised that if he could so easily feel the cancer why couldn't he just pluck it out and send me on my way. I guess my mental state was such that a bit of fanciful dreaming was necessary to minimise the seriousness of my health problem. After all, wishful thinking is something we all engage in at times. Had I been writing a piece of science fiction then this scenario may have been exactly what was required. Alas this wasn't science fiction and I quickly returned to the reality of my situation.

The reality as presented by the surgeon was that I required surgery and I needed it as soon as possible. The cancer had been there for some time (possibly years), slowly growing in size. However the positive news as indicated by the scans was that the cancer had not moved outside the rectum into other parts of the body. This would simplify the surgery and would minimise the chances of cancer returning in the future. At this point in the discussion a model was used to show me where the cancer was located and what would be required to remove it. Maybe, like me, you were unaware that the rectum is located between the anus and the colon (large intestine), that it is about 20 centimetres long, and important in controlling the release of faeces.

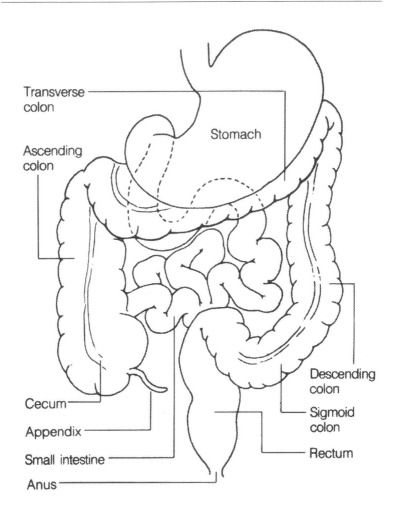

Illustration of Gastrointestinal System
(National Cancer Institute Visuals Online)

Rectal cancers typically grow slowly so mine was not unusual. The first stage is usually as a precancerous growth called a polyp. If the polyp becomes cancerous it firstly grows in the lining of the rectum (epithelium) and then as it develops it grows into the deeper layers of the rectum. It was clear from the size of my cancer that it had indeed been there for a long time.

The discussion seemed a little unreal to me. There were moments when I felt as though we were talking about some other person. I guess this reflected a measure of my disbelief that this was happening to me, or possibly a denial that I had cancer or simply my way of dealing with the grim facts about surgery – about being cut open and having something cut out of me. After all, I was fit and had never taken a single day's sick leave from work in over 25 years. My friends saw me as the fittest and healthiest person they knew. My identity had become that of a fit and healthy person. They often joked about this at my expense. Now everyone would know that I was not indestructible and that I had cancer. I continued to have irrational thoughts about my situation including shutting my eyes so that this bad dream might go away and I might awake cancer-free.

At this point in the consultation the surgeon reiterated that his advice was for me to have surgery as soon as possible. While I had come to the conclusion in my mind that surgery was inevitable the thought of having it sooner rather than later was something I was now being confronted with. I had only recently found out that I had cancer and now I was being asked to consent to have surgery as soon as possible. My thoughts turned to contemplating what it might mean and what exactly it would involve. And what about after the surgery? If everything went well, how soon after surgery would I be able to run?

We started to explore these questions. It was explained that in my case there were some plusses. Firstly it appeared from the scans that the cancer had not spread beyond the rectum. Secondly it was located at the back of the rectum, which apparently was good. Thirdly I was thin and this would make the surgery much simpler (I had little fat tissue to cut through which, according to the surgeon, would make the procedure easier). Fourthly I was very fit and this would assist in my recovery.

Even with these plusses the surgery would be complex and

would probably take some three to four hours. I was surprised by the time it would take (after all in my earlier day dreaming a simple plucking would only take a few minutes). However the reality was much different. I was advised that the surgery would involve a long vertical incision in the front extending from just below the sternum to just above the pubic area. After making the incision most parts that lay inside (bladder, blood vessels, tendons, intestines) would need to be moved aside to allow access to the rectum. This was clearly not something that could be undertaken in a hurry.

I was told that with all surgery there are some risks and clearly the more complex the surgery the greater the risks. However this process was something that the surgeon had done many times and so I had no doubts about his ability to do the operation. I was also advised that there may well be an adverse reaction by some parts of the body as a result of being handled. For example my libido may be reduced or there may be difficulties with bladder functioning. Lastly I was advised that a temporary ileostomy would be created during the surgery in order to allow the rectum to heal. An ileostomy is a surgical opening constructed by bringing the end or loop of small intestine (the ileum) out onto the surface of the skin. Intestinal waste passes out of the ileostomy and is collected in an external pouching system stuck to the skin. Ileostomies are usually sited above the groin on the right-hand side of the abdomen, which is where the surgeon advised me he would locate my ileostomy. This meant I would wear an ileostomy bag for about four months and then I would require further surgery to reverse the process. I would apparently be in hospital for two weeks.

I sat silently for a few moments trying to mentally recap and fully comprehend all that I had been told. It was clear that I needed surgery, that it should be as soon as possible, the surgery would be complex and long, many of my internal parts would be moved around during the surgery, some of those parts won't like being touched and may react adversely and I would need to wear a temporary ileostomy bag after the surgery. While the surgeon spoke confidently and reassuringly, I still needed to take a deep breath or two to absorb what I had been told.

This seemed like an appropriate place for a commercial break. Hence there was a pause during which we sat looking at one another before the surgeon started the conversation again by commenting that I clearly was fit because of my regular exercise. At this point, possibly as a way of breaking the silence and lightening the conversation, he enquired about the level of exercise that I undertook. I explained that I was a runner, that I ran each morning and that I had been running for about 30 years.

Before he could comment Penny added: 'He runs marathons'. 'Oh,' said the surgeon, 'and when do you plan to run your next one?' In retrospect, this was a strange question for the surgeon to ask but it just came out. For a moment I wasn't sure what to say but finally I blurted out: 'Sunday'. It was the surgeon's turn for a pause and he then said: 'This Sunday?' (which was three days hence). I had fleeting thoughts about the possible consequence of answering yes but I finally nodded my head. I really wanted to run this one. I had trained hard for three months. I was part of a group and we were all supporting one another. I didn't want to be told that I shouldn't do it. It may sound bizarre after what I had just been told about the proposed surgery, but emotionally I needed to compete in this event. The surgeon asked a couple of questions about the event and I then asked the question that I could no longer avoid. What did he think about me running 42.2 kilometres on Sunday? There was a look of puzzlement and disbelief on his face. He eventually said that he had never been asked that question before and really didn't know what to advise. Following a further pause he added that it would probably be okay, but he would leave the decision to me. I felt a great sense of relief because I wasn't advised not to compete in the marathon.

It was time to leave, having agreed that I would proceed with the surgery and that I would phone him on Monday to see if he had news about a date for the surgery. Monday morning arrived and, like many work mornings, it was busy. I had been asked to provide urgent written advice on a matter within my area of responsibility and expertise. I used the business of the morning to avoid making the telephone call to the surgeon. Normally I would have provided some direction to my team and then left them to get on with the briefing. However on this morning I involved myself in the task. It took my mind to another place and delayed that telephone call. The task was finally completed and thus it was time to make the call. The receptionist answered and I cleared my throat and asked to speak to the surgeon. He was soon on the phone and immediately wanted to know if I ran the marathon. I told him that I had. He then wanted to know how I fared and I told him that I had done well, coming second in my age group with a faster time than the previous year. He wanted to know how I felt. 'My legs are tired and sore and I have trouble with stairs', I said.

I didn't tell him that finishing had been a very emotional experience for me that had included shedding some tears. Instead I took a deep breath and asked him if he had any success in finding a time for my surgery. He replied that he had and asked: 'How would 25 April suit you?'. Anzac Day, a public holiday. I thought that seems like a strange date to pick. I would normally be participating in the Anzac Day relays – an annual event involving many teams of runners. It was only nine days away. I eventually replied that 25 April would be fine. He wanted to know if I had any questions. I had no questions because all I could think of was that the surgery was only nine days away. My mind then went into overdrive thinking about all the things I needed to attend to in the next nine days.

Two days later I completed the hospital admission papers and signed a form for the doctor indicating that I was aware of the purpose of the surgery and agreed to it being undertaken. The following day I was required to attend the pre-admission clinic at the hospital for a blood test, electrocardiogram, X-ray and some other tests and measurements. I received more information about the surgery and the workings of the hospital were explained to me. I was now ready for the surgery. I walked out of the hospital feeling very strange and thinking this is all a little unreal. I had completed a marathon only four days previously and my test results at the hospital were those of a healthy fit person. However, I would return to this place in a few days to be cut open so that a cancer could be removed.

Chapter 3

Anzac Day

Up there Cazaly, in there and fight, Out there and at 'em show 'em your might. Up there Cazaly, don't let 'em in, Fly like an angel, you're out there to win.

Up There Cazaly. Mike Brady[1]

Anzac Day (25 April) in Australia and New Zealand is a day of recollection and reflection. A day when those who lost their lives in war are acknowledged and the sacrifice they made is remembered. It has also increasingly become a day of some introspection by the nation; an important public holiday and one of the parts of the national narrative. For me this Anzac Day would be different and I would probably remember it and reflect on it in future for a very different reason. The memories of the Anzacs include many stories of courage and bravery. I had thought much about my cancer and the impending surgery and these thoughts included some negative fearful thoughts about the unknown. I had resolved each time I had

---

[1] Although the words 'Up There Cazaly' were initially associated with Australian Rules football they passed into more common use and according to Geoffrey Dutton (Australian Heroes) they were used during World War II as a greeting, an encouragement and a show of triumph.

such thoughts to have courage, which for me was about acting and trusting in spite of any fear. It was time for me to be tested as to how well I would handle the procedures leading to surgery, the surgery and the consequences of the surgery. Having never had surgery before, or indeed been in hospital, this was a new experience for me.

It was almost 10.30 am when we walked into the hospital for me to be admitted. My surgery was scheduled for about midday and so I needed to be there about two hours earlier to settle in and receive pre-surgery preparation. The admission process was quick and I was soon on my way to the surgical ward. Penny was with me, as well as two of my adult children, Fleur and Josh, as additional support.

Although I felt calm and joked with my family, my blood pressure reading was that of someone under stress. Clearly things were a little different on the inside. My mind wandered occasionally to thinking about what this experience really would be like and how much pain would be involved. I also had thoughts about my running friends participating in the Anzac Day relays (something I would usually be doing).

We were ushered into a waiting room at first, as my room was not ready. A nurse was soon asking me a number of questions all of which I had answered when completing the admission forms and again at my pre-admission interview. Did I have any of a long list of diseases or medical conditions? Was I allergic to anything? What was my date of birth? Who was my doctor? Was that my signature? At least answering this long list of questions kept me from thinking about the surgery.

My room was soon ready and so we all moved in to inspect what would be my home for the next two weeks. We agreed that it was a nice room and that it would be fine for a two-week stay. It even had a view (of the car park). I held up my hospital gown, a garment that I would become very familiar with. Some jokes were made about how wonderful I would look wearing it and how the split down the back would assist in keeping me cool.

I stood in the room holding the gown and wondering when I

should change into it when two people suddenly entered the room. The first person introduced herself as the anaesthetist and the other was a wardsman. They had come to take me to the theatre. The anaesthetist said: 'They are running a little ahead of schedule and are ready for you now'. 'Oh,' I thought, 'it's time already'. I could feel my heart rate increase a little. However, there was no time to think as I needed to quickly change into the hospital gown and get into the bed and then we were on our way. We were soon into the elevator and down to the ground floor where the theatres were located. The anaesthetist walked next to me and talked to me assuring me that she would be with me all the way through the surgery; that she would be looking after me and monitoring my body functions closely. This was our first meeting and I was immediately impressed by her reassuring and competent manner. She gave the impression that she cared about me.

My family had followed down the stairs and along the corridor to the doors that led into an area where the operating theatres were located. There was time for a quick pause in the procession for some hugs and kisses before I disappeared through the doors. My bed was now on the other side of those large double doors and I was now separate from Penny and family.

I fortunately had little time to think or be anxious as I was immediately greeted by a nurse, who proceeded to ask me a series of questions: what was my name, my doctor's name, my date of birth, and the purpose of the surgery. I clearly passed the test as my bed was quickly on the move through another door and into a long corridor. This corridor led to a series of theatres. My bed stopped at Theatre Number 4 and a door automatically opened and then closed after the bed had entered. This was a small preparation room, large enough for the bed, some equipment and some cupboards around the walls. There was space for a person on each side of the bed. My surgeon entered the room from the theatre, where he had been operating, dressed in a theatre gown and cap with a mask dangling around his neck. He greeted me, asked if I was okay and if I had any questions, touched me on the shoulder and indicated that I was in the hands of a good team.

The anaesthetist was now holding my hand and talking about her role. She again said that she would be closely monitoring my progress. While stroking my hand she took a razor and shaved some hair from the back of my right hand and from parts of my arm. She explained that she would use three points from which to monitor what was happening with me. She then pointed to where she would place the three cannulas (tubes that have a needle at the end). She would put the first one into my wrist. As she explained this she prepared the skin for the insertion of the first one. 'You will feel a slight sting', she said as she inserted the first needle. This was followed by a process of taping the cannula in place. This process was one that I would become very familiar with over the months to follow. She then proceeded to inject a substance into the cannula and continued to talk to me. I was soon asleep and so didn't get to see the completion of her work or the inside of the theatre.

I next remember being spoken to by someone. 'Mr Limbrick, hello. Mr Limbrick are you awake?' The room seemed very dim. The voice had come from a nurse who introduced herself and told me that the surgery was over and I was in the ICU. It was by now late in the afternoon but felt like it was the middle of the night. The nurse recorded my temperature, heart rate, blood pressure and oxygen uptake from the monitor I was connected to. She informed me that I was connected to a unit that contained morphine, which I could self-administer by pushing a button. 'Don't put up with any pain,' she advised me, 'simply push the button'. Although the room seemed very dim due to my fuzzy state there were in fact many lights turned on in the ICU.

Soon after the nurse finished with me Penny arrived. How wonderful it was to see her. She kissed me and gave me a hug (the kind you give someone who has just had major surgery, is connected to a monitor by several wires, has an intravenous drip, is wearing a catheter connected to a bag and who is now wearing an ileostomy bag). 'How are you darling?' she asked. I was okay, very tired but no pain at that point. She told me that the surgeon had telephoned her, was pleased with the surgery and said there had been no unexpected difficulties. I don't remember much about the remainder of that day or night. Due to a combination of the anaesthetic and some morphine I was very sleepy and dozed a lot. I recall waking a number of times not really knowing what time it was (the lights were always on in the ICU). I remember another patient calling several times and insisting that the nurses telephone his wife to come and collect him. Clearly from their response he thought he was in better shape than they did.

The following morning I woke to find Penny by my bedside. She was making a quick visit as part of her early morning run (she is also a runner). What a wonderful surprise. I was only supposed to be in the ICU for one night and then back to my room in the surgical ward the following morning. However, the specialist in charge of the ICU decided that I needed close monitoring for a little longer, possibly for another night. Penny returned a little later in the morning bringing lots of messages from family and friends. I tried to listen as she read out the messages to me but kept fading in an out because of my sleepy state. We were soon joined by my surgeon, who quickly looked at his handiwork, talked a little about the surgery and seemed pleased with the result. His visits, which usually took place at about 7 o'clock each morning, became part of the daily routine while I was in hospital.

I was extremely thirsty and badly wanted a drink and became somewhat possessed with the desire to drink. I had a mental picture of a glass of cold water, which I so badly wanted to drink. However I had been told that I was a 'nil by mouth' patient, but as a special concession I would be allowed to have a few ice cubes. The first one was magic. It tasted like the best 'drink' I had ever had. I vowed that I would never again take a glass of water for granted. How difficult it must be for those who don't have access to a tap that gives clean drinking water.

I experienced some discomfort and the occasional sharp pain as I adjusted my position in bed. A nurse arrived and said that I had to get out of bed, sit for a short time and then walk across the room before returning to bed. My first thought about this direction was don't be silly I can't get up and walk. I had visions of doing damage to the areas that had been cut and stitched up. Sitting up seemed daunting enough. I was very apprehensive about the wisdom of this. However I was given no choice and two nurses were soon hovering to get me onto my feet and into a nearby chair. They suggested that I might consider administering a shot of morphine before the move started. I agreed because I wasn't sure of the level of pain that I might experience. The various tubes, wires and bags connected to me had to be repositioned before I could be moved. With this done, I took a deep breath, and then was quickly moved to the upright position on the bed. I felt some discomfort and was then swung around and my feet lowered to the floor. With a little more help and some further encouragement I was standing unsteadily on the floor. With a pause and a nurse on each side I was encouraged to walk to the chair. Just a few days back I had run a marathon and now I was having difficulty walking a couple of metres.

Following a few very shaky steps I arrived at the chair. 'Now, how do I turn around and sit?' I wondered. The process was controlled by the nurses who expertly twisted me around and down in a single movement. A sharp but quick pain and I was now sitting. After about an hour (it seemed much longer) the process was repeated in reverse but involved a slightly longer walk. As I moved I was followed by a number of tubes and wires connected to various bits of equipment and some bags. Walking around with a drip, tubes, wires and bags was something that I would do many times during my stay in hospital (often with my hospital gown flapping open at the back).

At 4 o'clock that afternoon I was told that it had been decided that I could go to the surgical ward. I saw this as a positive move and a step in my recovery. It also meant that I would be disconnected from some of the apparatus that I was connected to, which was found only in the ICU.

On the two days after my surgery I felt only minor discomfort and occasional pain (quickly controlled by the morphine, which I was using less and less). I continued to be very sleepy, falling asleep frequently (often in the middle of a conversation). I think this was partly due to the occasional use of morphine and partly due to the impact of the surgery. I was pleased that I was recovering so quickly without any major discomfort. The level of pain that I imagined might accompany major surgery never eventuated. I had a large number of visitors and was pleased to see them, although I had difficulty staying awake (it was good that Penny was present to continue the conversations).

On the night of the second day after the surgery the situation changed rather dramatically. I had a night of little sleep and felt dreadful – both physically and mentally. My stomach was inflated and my abdomen was extremely tight and uncomfortable. Over the next few days this feeling persisted and I vomited a number of times. I felt exhausted after each episode. Mentally I had dark thoughts. These thoughts were alien to me as I was an optimistic, cheerful person. After feeling so good initially I couldn't understand what was happening. Then I found out that this was a fairly normal reaction after the type of surgery that I had undergone. Many of the components found in my abdomen (organs, blood vessels, tendons) had been handled during the surgery in order to get to the cancer. Their response was to shut down and to stop working. They had apparently gone into a state of shock. It was clear that I would continue to feel dreadful until they had overcome the shock and progressively start to work again. After six days I started to feel a little better and I gradually improved each day, although those few days seemed like a very long time.

After normality started to return I was allowed to commence eating again. Up to that point it was only able to have a few ice cubes. This was an exciting time for someone who enjoys food and who loves cooking delicious things to eat. I was destined to be disappointed. My first food was called 'clear fluids', which bore little resemblance to the food that I remembered from only about a week ago. I was able to choose between clear chicken, beef or vegetable soup. I sampled all three over the next couple of days. They looked like water that had been coloured and had a mild warm salty flavour. I was offered clear fruit juice to accompany the meal. Over the next week I progressed slowly towards solid food.

My daily routine usually involved a blood test early in the morning, followed by a visit from my surgeon, then breakfast (after I was allowed to eat) and an assisted shave and shower. I was then ready for a compulsory walk, which required some preparation including getting my saline drip and three bags in place (urine, wound drainage and ileostomy). After a 'lap' around the ward I was exhausted and needed to sit or lie down. I was encouraged to stay out of bed for as long as possible and hence to sit rather than lie. However, sitting was extremely uncomfortable because my backside ached as a consequence of the surgery on my rectum. I tried standing but found this very tiring. It was impossible to completely escape the constant ache in my backside.

I didn't enjoy nights in the hospital. They involved little sleep, which was not my normal pattern, as I had always slept very soundly. I thus spent most nights listening to music, watching TV, viewing movies on an iPod or reading. One night I watched the movie *Happy Feet* on an iPod. This was exactly the kind of feel-good movie that I needed at that time. It made me feel like dancing and I thought about my happy feet running. The nights seemed very long and provided time for the occasional period of negative thinking (some self-talk usually fixed this). I was visited a couple of times during the night by a nurse who would do my 'obs' (observations–temperature, blood pressure, oxygen uptake) and ask if I had any pain. 'Tell me what your pain is like on a scale of 0 to 10' was a question I was asked many times. I had asked for the morphine to be removed on the fourth day after the surgery and from that time onwards had been given paracetamol periodically for my aching backside.

Very soon after my surgery two of my running friends presented me with books. The first one to arrive was *It's Not About the Bike. My Journey Back to Life*, by Lance Armstrong, and the second one to arrive was *3:59.4. The Quest to Break the 4 Minute Mile*, by John Bryant. I found both books inspirational in different ways. Armstrong's fight with cancer resonated with me and I found the determination shown over a long period of time to break the four-minute mark for the mile to be very meaningful. It's interesting that 1953–54 marked the conquest of two seemingly impossible peaks: Mount Everest and the four-minute mile. During the 'long' nights I was able to lose myself in these stories and associate with the achievements recorded in both books. Although recent revelations about drug taking by Lance Armstrong have been unfortunate and disappointing, I was at that time most interested in his battle with cancer, the treatment, the pain and the determination to cycle again. This reinforced my determination to beat cancer and to get back to running. I came back to these stories in my mind many times as my treatment progressed.

During the first week of my stay in hospital a nurse had largely tended to my ileostomy. A small bag was attached to my abdomen on the right side and it drained into a much larger bag, which the nurses emptied periodically. During the second week of my hospitalisation I was visited by a specialist nurse who indicated that it was time for me to start taking care of my ileostomy. This would involve draining the bag whenever it was full and removing it completely every three to four days and replacing it with a new one (I was given a single piece bag and plate to use but would use other types as time went on). This was a new phase in taking control, which I had been able to largely ignore up to that point. I was given a demonstration by the specialist nurse in removing the bag, cleaning the skin, applying protective coating from a wipe, cutting a hole on the bag base to fit neatly over the ileostomy and then applying the new bag after having first removed a barrier to expose a sticky base. The following day the nurse returned and it was my turn to go through the process under her direction. It was now up to me to take care of my ileostomy.

I was also progressively being relieved of tubes and leads, which had connected me to various pieces of apparatus, to bags and the IV drip. The first time this happened was on leaving the ICU, which halved the number of connections. The next to go was a drain that was inserted into my abdomen and went to the site of the surgery. It had been draining blood into a bag. 'Now take a deep breath,' the nurse said as she quickly pulled the tube out. The small hole that this left in my side was covered with a dressing and all was well until I stood to go for a walk and found that after a few steps I had blood running down my legs and the front of my gown was turning red. I immediately thought I had disturbed something inside that had been stitched. However, it was only a blood clot that had formed inside and burst delivering the contents over me. The next tube to go was the catheter that drained my bladder. 'Now take a deep breath,' was again the instruction. It was gone and so was another bag. The last to go was the IV drip that by now had started to annoy me. Although the site of the cannula had been changed several times the existing site was sore and I was tired of wheeling the drip around every time I moved away from the bed. Having the cannula removed and being free of the drip gave me a great sense of freedom and recovery.

During my stay in hospital I spent lots of time looking out from my first floor window at the world below. I could watch people arrive and depart. I imagined who they might be and why they were at the hospital. I could see my doctor arrive each morning. I was able to observe hospital staff taking a break and having a cigarette at various hospital exits. This made me feel disappointed at first and progressively I was angry with them for not taking care of their health. I speculated at what damage they might be doing to their bodies. If they only realised what pain and discomfort they might be consigning themselves to. I felt like shouting out to warn them and to tell them what had happened to a fit person who hadn't smoked. I of course know that people don't change their habits until they are ready to do so and hence my calling out would have had no impact (although, it may have provided some amusement). It's interesting to speculate on how many hospital staff smoke regardless of the fact that they deal daily with people who are sick and in many cases in pain (possibly because of smoking). Seeing these people smoke had an impact on me at that time possibly because I was affected emotionally by what I had experienced.

I had plenty of time to think while in hospital and my thoughts were frequently about running again. I often lamented missing my daily runs. They were such an integral and important part of my daily routine. Penny had brought in the latest edition of a running magazine (*Runners World*) that we subscribe to. The magazine always had stories about other runners (people of all ages and abilities, including some with disabilities). I found these stories about their achievements inspirational and hypnotic and read about new running adventures or trails, new tips to improve performance, foods and recipes and the latest running gear. I often relived past runs and fanaticised about future runs. The surgery was now over, I would soon be out of hospital and I was sure that in a week or two I would be back running again.

Chapter 4

Complications

Accept what comes to you totally and completely so that you can appreciate it, learn from it and then let it go.

Journey into Healing. Deepak Chopra

Two days after the surgery my surgeon advised me that as a precaution he had removed the adjoining lymph nodes when he removed the cancer. He indicated that they had been sent to the laboratory for testing along with the rectal cancer and that it would be about a week before the results were available. I had very quickly forgotten about that conversation. Then on the morning of the eighth day when he arrived for his usual morning visit he indicated that he had the laboratory results and they had shown that cancer cells were present in four of the lymph nodes. This news came at a time when I was feeling good about my recovery and looking forward to going home. It was a shock because the scans had shown no trace of cancer outside the muscle tissue of the rectum. Clearly my state of surprise and shock was evident to the surgeon as he quickly added that he was confident that he had removed all traces of the cancer. The bad news was that I would now have to undergo a period of chemotherapy and radiotherapy and would need to retain the temporary ileostomy until this treatment had been completed. I needed to quickly adjust to this news, accept it and move on in my thinking about my treatment.

I of course now know much more about rectal cancer and the stages of its development and given the length of time my cancer had been present it's not surprising that it had moved outside the rectum wall. I am fortunate that it had not moved beyond the lymph nodes.

As I mentioned previously there are a number of stages in the development of colorectal or bowel cancer. They are as follows:

- Stage 0: Very early cancer on the innermost layer of the intestine
- Stage 1: Cancer is in the inner layers of the colon/rectum
- Stage 2: Cancer has spread through the muscle wall of the colon/rectum
- Stage 3: Cancer has spread to the lymph nodes
- Stage 4: Cancer has spread to other organs

Hence the laboratory results that the doctor had received demonstrated that I now had to deal with a Stage 3 and not a Stage 2 cancer and this clearly would involve a more complex and lengthy treatment regimen.

I was interested to find out why I would need both chemotherapy and radiotherapy. It seems that they work in different ways with the chemotherapy designed to destroy cancerous cells and the radiotherapy designed to destroy cancerous tissue. Hence having the two types of therapy increases the likelihood that any remaining cancer will be eliminated.

It was now clear that my treatment would no longer be over in about four months and further surgery would have to wait until the chemotherapy/radiotherapy program had been completed. I was now confronted with a set of new challenges and decisions. The first of which was to select an oncologist for the chemotherapy treatment and to commence the treatment no later than five weeks after the surgery that I had undergone about a week previously.

Having spent two weeks in hospital it was time to say goodbye to the nurses who had provided such good care and to move to the next phase of my treatment and recovery. The focus was now on regaining my strength and finding out more about my program of chemotherapy and radiotherapy. I had virtually no understanding of what these processes would involve.

Following the surgery and my stay in hospital I felt remarkably tired. This was a new experience for me. I had always slept well and rarely slept during the day. However I now had difficulty getting through the day without an afternoon sleep and I sometimes slept soundly for as much as two hours. This tiredness also affected my ability to move about as my legs lacked the strength they had before surgery. I thus spent lots of time sitting and then trying to get some exercise by walking about the living area of our house. After coming home my running friends continued to offer help and support. About a week after discharge they organised to come to our place on a Friday afternoon to celebrate my return home. They arrived in force with some bottles of fine red wine and stayed for a couple of hours. The group stood around talking loudly, with me as the focus of attention. It was a wonderful gesture and made me feel special. However, when they departed I was exhausted. I hadn't stood for that length of time since the surgery and so my legs ached afterwards and I collapsed onto our lounge unable to move. It was clearly going to take a little bit of time for me to get back some strength and stamina. After this experience I started to think that perhaps I wouldn't be back to running for a few weeks yet.

Three weeks after leaving hospital I started my chemotherapy. I was still lacking in energy and felt tired and sore. I continued to have discomfort from my backside and so sitting for any length of time was difficult. I was also frustrated by an anal discharge, which was both uncomfortable and annoying. I had asked my surgeon if he could do something to stop it and he assured me that this was 'normal' and would stop at some point (he couldn't say when that would be but was confident that it would eventually stop). It persisted for about nine weeks, which I found very tiresome and frustrating. Occasionally there was also some bleeding. It was uncomfortable but I had to learn to live with it. Interestingly one day it just stopped and I felt a great sense of relief and freedom. I immediately felt like a different person as though an enormous advance had been made in my recovery. No more wet underwear or soggy pads.

Prior to commencing the chemotherapy I had selected an oncologist, with the help of a friend in the medical profession. The oncologist had agreed to accept me and hence our first meeting was arranged. Prior to our meeting he had carefully examined my records and after a brief discussion and an examination he indicated that I would require a program of treatment which would extend over a period of six months and would need to be undertaken in conjunction with radiotherapy at the midpoint in the chemotherapy program. The combined program was referred to as 5-Fluorouracil (5FU) with radiotherapy. The midpoint in the chemotherapy would involve a five-week period of continuous infusion of the 5FU and the radiotherapy would be given during that period.

My chemotherapy was provided at a private hospital within an oncology unit. An appointment was made for me to visit the unit and discuss my treatment with one of the oncology nurses. During the appointment I was able to view the main treatment room (where I saw a number of people sitting in chairs receiving chemotherapy). The discussion with the oncology nurse enabled me to receive more detailed information about the treatment, to receive information about possible side effects and to have the 'protocol' schedule associated with 5FU treatment explained to me. I was advised that the schedule would be as follows:

- Weeks 1 and 5:   intravenous chemotherapy each day for five days
- Weeks 9 to 13:   five weeks continuous infusion of chemotherapy concurrently with daily radiotherapy
- Weeks 17 and 21: intravenous chemotherapy for five days.

The three-week gaps between treatments were necessary to enable my immune system to recover sufficiently before the next treatment commenced. This is necessary because the chemotherapy destroys the body's blood cells.

Because the protocol involved a five-week period of continuous chemotherapy infusion in the middle of the schedule it was explained to me that I would need to have in place either a Picc line or a Portacath to receive the treatment. In other words I would be having the treatment 24 hours a day for the five weeks and it would not be possible to do this via a cannula at the oncology unit. It was also not possible to leave the hospital with a cannula in one of my veins. Hence I had to make a choice of the method I would use to have the five weeks of infusion. Would it be a Picc line or Portacath?

The Picc (peripherally inserted central catheter) line would involve having a catheter (i.e. a long flexible tube) inserted into one of the large veins in one of my arms with the aid of a local anaesthetic. The catheter is inserted into the vein until it sits in a large vein just above the heart. At the end of the line, which is outside the body, there is a special cap to which a drip line or syringe can be connected. I was advised that there can sometimes be problems with Picc lines, including infections, blood clots, air bubbles in the line, and a break or cut in the line. The external part of the catheter is held in place with a dressing that would require changing each week.

The Portacath on the other hand has two components: a reservoir (the portal) and a tube (the catheter). The portal is implanted in the upper chest under the skin and is probably visible as a small bump. The catheter, which is attached to the portal, runs in a tunnel under the skin, going over the collarbone and then into a large vein in the lower neck (the internal jugular vein). The septum of the portal is made of a special self-sealing silicone rubber and can be punctured up to 1000 times (and so can be used many times over a number of years). To use the Portacath the skin over it is sterilised and the port is accessed by puncturing the overlying skin with a special needle (known as a Huber needle). Some blood is then normally withdrawn using a syringe to ensure that it's operating normally and then it is flushed with saline followed by heparin to prevent clotting. The implant of the Portacath would require day surgery. I was advised that problems with a Portacath are rare but they sometimes occur and can include blood clotting and infection.

The infusion process would involve connection to a small pump, which would be with me for the five-week period, 24 hours a day. The pump, which would be in a small case, could be worn with a shoulder strap and would deliver a dose of chemotherapy at predetermined intervals. I would need to attend the hospital each week to have the pump checked and to have it loaded with a new container of chemotherapy.

I departed with further written information about both the Picc line and Portacath and was asked to consider both and make a decision about which method I would select. This was a decision that I did not need to make immediately because it would be a number of weeks before I needed to have the chemotherapy by continuous infusion. In the meantime I could attend the hospital daily and have a cannula inserted into a vein so that I could receive my daily dose. However, it was pointed out to me that I could start using the Picc line or Portacath as soon the one I chose was in place. This made me think that having one in place as soon as possible would be an advantage if it avoided the daily cannula routine. My experience in hospital was that my wrists and hands became sore quickly from having a cannula in place.

The day for my first chemotherapy came quickly. I was advised to attend the oncology unit any time on the Monday morning between 10 am and 12 noon. I arrive at 10 am and was allocated a large armchair in a room containing many such chairs place around the walls of the room (possibly 20 chairs). Most of the chairs were occupied by people receiving chemotherapy. I carefully looked around the room at each of the individuals and concluded that many of them looked unwell. The nurses were very attentive, supportive and cheerful, and smiled frequently. Although this was a room full of sick people the atmosphere was positive and buoyant.

A nurse came to me and asked which hand I preferred to use for the chemotherapy today. It didn't really matter because the other hand would be used the following day. I was a little apprehensive. Not because of the need to have a cannula but because I was about to receive a dose of chemotherapy and I was aware that it would have some side effects. Being right handed I selected my left hand and it was briefly rubbed to warm it which helped get the blood vessels to stand out a little more. It was then sterilised and the cannula quickly inserted and taped in place. I discovered over the remainder of the week that the nurses in this unit were very proficient at inserting a cannula with minimum discomfort. I am also fortunate in having large blood vessels from running for many years (a doctor friend once commented that you could drive a truck up them). However, despite the excellent treatment, by the end of the week the backs of my hands were sore.

The next part of the process involved connecting me to a saline drip to ensure that I was well hydrated while having the chemotherapy. I was also offered water and fruit juice to drink. After about 30 minutes it was time to receive my first chemotherapy. It was clear that some people were receiving their chemotherapy from a bag, which had replaced the drip. However, my 5FU came in a very large syringe, which was administered via the tube that carried the saline drip. The nurse administering the chemotherapy was dressed in protective clothing, gloves and glasses, and sat in front of me while very slowly administering the chemotherapy. I recall feeling hot (like a hot flush) but I think this was probably caused more through apprehension than by the chemotherapy.

Following the chemotherapy I was left to receive the remainder of the bag of saline drip. At that point I was given an injection of an anti-emetic to reduce any feeling of nausea. I returned each day that week and went through the same routine.

I was advised that possible side effects could range from mild nausea through to severe diarrhoea, skin rashes, mouth ulcers, gritty eyes, tiredness and temperature elevation. I was also told that the side effects might increase as the chemotherapy progressed.

During that week a community nurse visited me at home as a follow-up to my surgery and as potential support during my chemotherapy. This did mean that I would have additional support and advice, including an emergency telephone number to call if I encountered problems after hours. She gave me advice on handling side effects, including the use of ginger to help with nausea. As a result I consumed lots of ginger beer over the next six months. I was also told that I needed to take my temperature each night and if it exceeded a particular point then I had to phone the number I was given and probably go to hospital. Each night Penny and I went through a routine of taking my temperature and, although it was close to the critical point several times, we never had to phone the emergency number.

Following the experience of a week of chemotherapy I decided that I needed to quickly decide on an alternative to having the daily cannula. During my week at the oncology unit each day I had observed a number of people receiving chemotherapy via a Portacath and a few via a Picc line. Based on my observations, some questions that I asked of the nurses and looking at the advantages and disadvantages of the two methods I decided that the Portacath was the one for me. It would after all be out of sight when not in use – unlike the Picc line, which would involve having a piece of tubing taped to your arm.

I now had a three-week window before my next chemotherapy,

which I felt could be an opportunity to have a Portacath installed. The oncology unit had provided me with the details of surgeons that had experience in Portacath installation. I was fortunate in being able to quickly arrange an appointment, which resulted in a decision to install the device via day surgery on a Monday seven days before my next round of chemotherapy was due to commence. Unfortunately my regular blood test on the Friday before the Monday of the surgery indicated that my white blood cell count was too low to permit surgery. The surgery was rescheduled for Friday in the hope that my cell count would improve sufficiently. A further blood test on the Wednesday found that it was up from just above 0 to 50 per cent of normal. This was deemed adequate for the Portacath surgery to proceed.

I felt enormously relieved that the surgery could proceed as planned. Clearly if my blood cell count hadn't recovered sufficiently this time I would be faced with the same problem after my second week of chemotherapy. As I needed to have the Portacath installed before the third round of chemotherapy (i.e. the five-week continuous infusion) this would mean that there would need to be a halt to my chemotherapy program until the blood count had risen sufficiently. I was extremely keen to receive my chemotherapy without any delays in the program, as I saw each treatment as another step towards full recovery.

Friday arrived and I presented to the day surgery unit at the hospital at 7 am. The procedure went very smoothly and I recovered quickly from the general anaesthetic. I was kept under observation until late in the afternoon and then finally allowed to go home with my Portacath in place in the right side of my chest. I had gained another incision and a number of stitches that would need to be removed at some stage.

The next week of chemotherapy went smoothly using my new Portacath. No sore hands at the end of that week. Having the Portacath in place also sped up the chemotherapy process. It meant that a needle could be quickly inserted into the Portacath (involving a slight sting in my chest) and then the process was underway.

By the end of my second week of chemotherapy I was surprised that there was no noticeable increase in the level and intensity of the side effects from chemotherapy. The main difficulty was continuous low-level nausea. It was present all the time, although rarely reaching a level that necessitated me taking the nausea tablets that I'd been given at the commencement of the treatment. I just kept drinking ginger beer in large quantities and eating dried ginger (I occasionally had a special treat: ginger chocolate). I also had gritty eyes lots of the time and I had some mouth ulcers and rashes and was generally tired.

By the completion of my second round of chemotherapy I had recovered sufficiently from my surgery to start a program of walking in order to try and regain some of my fitness and get some strength back into my legs. Walking quickly became an important part of my daily routine. At first I could only walk for about 10 minutes, but, with commitment and determination, I progressively increased this to 90 minutes a day. I didn't want to lose any more of my fitness and saw walking as an essential step in getting my fitness back and hopefully moving me closer to running again. In my mind my life would not be back to normal until I was again running. Although the chemotherapy increased my level of tiredness I was determined to get back my pre-surgery level of fitness and I felt that being fit would assist me to handle the chemotherapy with minimal problems. I was also convinced that it would contribute to a full recovery. Exercising would also be a distraction from the chemotherapy, which had become such a dominant part of my life and I badly wanted to get back into running as soon as possible.

I was now approaching the nine-week mark in my chemotherapy program, which had two implications for me. Firstly I would move to the five-week process of continuous infusion of chemotherapy. Secondly it also meant that my radiotherapy would start. Hence I would again be moving into new territory on both counts. I started to wonder how I would feel having continuous chemotherapy for five weeks and what radiotherapy would be like. Would the combination of the two treatments magnify the side effects?

However, before the start day for the radiotherapy I had to meet with an oncology doctor at the radiotherapy unit in a different hospital, but near to where I was having my chemotherapy. This was a fairly routine consultation and was followed by an appointment with a therapist in the radiotherapy unit.

The appointment with the therapist was similar to the chemotherapy interview I had before commencing my chemotherapy. I was asked a number of questions and given information about the process and about possible side effects (with an emphasis of the possibility of burning and blistering of my skin). I also had to be marked i.e. I had to have marks placed on my skin so that the radiotherapy could be delivered to exactly the same place each time. For this to happen a CT scan was used to pinpoint where the rectal cancer had been and using this as a reference point three marks were placed on my skin (one on each side in the hip area and a third in the pubic region). The marks were then made permanent by tattooing a small dot at each of these three points. I still have my three 'tattoos'.

Week 9 arrived and I received my little black box with the pump and chemotherapy and had it connected to the Portacath. I walked out of the chemotherapy unit with it slung over my shoulder and a catheter through my shirtfront to the Portacath in my chest. So far so good; only five weeks to go.

On that same morning I presented to the radiotherapy unit for my first radiotherapy treatment. I was fortunate as I lived close to both the chemotherapy and radiotherapy units, which were located in adjoining hospitals on the same campus and I could walk to both from my home and walk between the two units. A new routine started on that day with a 15-minute walk to the radiotherapy unit accompanied by my little black box of chemotherapy. This was to be the daily routine for the next five weeks. For me the walk was an opportunity for a little more exercise, which I felt was good for my wellbeing and also a way to assist in managing side effects. I also looked upon this as an excursion and an opportunity to talk to the nurses, the other staff and others waiting to receive their radiotherapy. I always imagined that I looked somewhat healthier than the others waiting for their treatment. This was most likely untrue but was probably an indication of my thinking about myself as not really being sick. Many of the other people I encountered waiting for treatment looked sick to me and I felt thankful that I was feeling so good.

As I entered the third week and the midpoint of this combined chemotherapy and radiotherapy treatment time seemed to be moving very slowly. My tiredness and nausea had increased a little and I had some burning and redness of my skin around my backside. To help with the skin problem I was required to have a salt bath each day and to then apply a cream that I had been given. I also had an increase in the frequency of occurrence of some of the other side effects (rashes, tired and sore eyes, sore mouth).

When the combined treatment started I had continued with my daily long walks. I had in fact started to jog a little during the walk for a few metres at first and then a little longer and more frequently during my walk. These few running steps felt awkward and uncoordinated, although they were only very short slow intervals. They were incredibly hard and I felt as though I had never run before. However, a major breakthrough occurred in the third week of my combined treatment when I decided to see if I could run for 30 minutes without stopping. This was to be a 15-minute jog away from my home and then 15 minutes back. I managed to shuffle my way through the 30 minutes without stopping. It was one of the hardest runs I had ever done but I experienced a wonderful feeling of achievement. I was once again a 'runner'. I repeated the same run the next day and it was still very hard. However I persisted and within a week I was running 7 kilometres a day. It felt great being back in the old routine of daily running. It was hard physically but great emotionally. As I was still undergoing the continuous chemotherapy this meant that I had to run with my little black box connected to my Portacath. This presented me with a challenge, as the little box was heavy and bobbed up and down with the running motion. I was thus forced to run holding the box in one hand. I often wondered what people I encountered on my run thought of this person running and holding onto a black box (an oversized Walkman perhaps?).

At last the five weeks were finally over and I could free myself of my black box and there were no more daily trips to the hospital for radiotherapy. I had become accustomed to having the black box with me 24 hours a day, including finding a way to shower with it and not get it wet and sleeping with it tucked under the pillow. I recall waking in the night several times and walking half asleep to the toilet only to be pulled back by the catheter attaching me to the black box (it had to come with me). The last couple of weeks of the five weeks of combined treatment seemed to pass very slowly. I also had some soreness of skin from the radiotherapy (thankfully no blistering). I was so grateful that I was back running, as this was a real psychological boost and a distraction from my treatment. I was able to think about running, which was far more preferable to thinking about chemotherapy or radiotherapy. This five-week period in my treatment finally came to an end and I felt that another significant milestone had been reached. On the Friday night that the five-week period concluded Penny and I celebrated with a glass (or two) of good Australian bubbly. I think we were not only celebrating achieving a milestone but also life and I was definitely celebrating my return to running. I was told by several friends that I was looking good. I had recovered from the surgery, regained lost weight and even regained a reasonable amount of my fitness. Aside from the side effects from the chemotherapy and radiotherapy, I was now feeling much closer to normal.

Penny and I are both downhill snow skiers and usually spend time at the snow during the ski season. We had not discussed skiing during the current season but had individually reached the conclusion that it would not be possible to go to the snow that year. However some friends had other ideas. We received a phone call from friends that we usually skied with asking us to consider coming to the snow the following week. They suggested we could simply come along and have a holiday, relax and forget about treatment for a few days. 'Why not?' we concluded. After all I was feeling well (apart from the treatment side effects which were manageable), my appetite was almost back to normal and I was clearly much fitter. A holiday at the snow would certainly be good and we could catch up with our friends Dianne and Steve. Hence we arranged accommodation in our ski lodge where the others would be staying for a couple of weeks. We elected to go for five days in the week prior to my fourth round of chemotherapy.

In the few days before our departure for the snow we started to think about taking the skis along just in case we wanted to try skiing. The idea of skiing was very appealing to me. It was such a wonderful feeling gliding down the hill in a magic environment, feeling so free and being 'normal'. It is also one of those activities that require you to be in the moment. To be mentally somewhere else while skiing will quickly lead to disaster. If I could ski this would involve total concentration on that activity. So we packed the car and headed for the snow taking our skis along just in case. On the drive to the snow we decided that I would try skiing and if it was too demanding we would simply have a short holiday at the snow with our friends.

The next morning I was riding up the mountain in a chairlift heading for one of the highest points on the ski field. Although I had been there many times before it was done with mixed feelings and a little bit of determination to make it work. I wanted my body (particularly my legs) to respond in a way that enabled me to be able to make those turns in the snow and glide smoothly to the bottom of the run (one of the longest at the resort).

We alighted from the chairlift, which required a ski-off around to the start of the run. This first bit was ok. The technical component happened without thinking (my subconscious was still working) and the physical aspect seemed to work. But would it last for the next kilometre to the bottom? We all paused, allowing some other skiers to go before us and then it was time to go. The next part involved navigating down a short but rather tricky steep slope, which I have skied many times before. Although I was a little tentative, I conquered the slope and was on my way! We stopped several times down the slope but everything seemed to be working and clearly the legs were holding up. Reaching the bottom of the run I felt great emotionally and the group smiled. They all wanted me to succeed just as they also wanted me to recover fully.

We stayed for five days and I managed to ski for three of those days, generally from about 9.30 am to about 4 pm, with a coffee stop in the morning and a lunch break at about 1.30 pm. I only encountered one problem, which was fairly minor. This was a difficulty with the temporary ileostomy bag. It sat at about the level of the waist on my ski pants, which meant that if it filled up while I was moving side to side and up and down skiing the pressure could cause a leak or a completed dislodgement of the bag. A leak did in fact occur on the first day, but I was carrying tape and was able to repair it without any major difficulty. To avoid the problem on subsequent days I used braces to hold my ski pants up and left the top of the waist undone. This couldn't be seen, as my ski jacket was long enough to cover the waist area. The ileostomy bag wasn't going to stop me from skiing.

After a nice few days at the snow, and a confidence-boost by being able to ski, we headed home and it was soon time for my fourth dose of chemotherapy. That week was largely uneventful with the usual side effects being present. I then had a three-week break before my last week of chemotherapy. A blood test on the Friday before the fifth treatment period revealed that my cell count was sufficiently high enough for the chemotherapy to proceed without delay. 'Wonderful!' I thought. Only one week to go until the six months is over. We had been invited to a ball on the Saturday following the

Friday that my treatment was to finish. It seemed that this would be a good way to celebrate the conclusion to the chemotherapy program with friends. After my last dose of chemotherapy on Friday morning I walked home slowly thinking to myself how wonderful life is, but at the same time feeling a slight sense of disbelief that the chemotherapy was finally over.

Saturday evening came quickly and we were dressing for the ball. It was formal so I had to dust off my dinner suit, dress shirt and bow tie. The shirt and suit were both a little big on me, as I still hadn't regained my normal weight. I didn't care how I looked as I was going to the ball to celebrate and have some fun. It was a great night with some great dance music, which Penny and I made good use of. I felt healthy and well. The celebration was shared with some special friends including Keith and David, who had both beaten cancer, and Richard, my marathon running partner. It was also appropriate that the ball was organised to raise funds for breast cancer support. We went home late and I was physically very tired but mentally in good shape. I slept very late the next morning.

With the chemotherapy over there remained only one step in the process: the reversal surgery to remove the temporary ileostomy and allow my system to work normally again. I now needed to discuss a date with my surgeon. This I planned to do on Monday morning.

Chapter 5

A Near-Death Experience

It's not that I am afraid of dying – I just don't want to be there when it happens.

Woody Allen

I had finished my treatment and so was ready to move on. I wanted to get back to normal life as soon as possible. Monday came and I was quickly on the phone to my surgeon. He was not inclined to rush the final surgery and felt some recovery time after chemotherapy was needed (particularly as my immune system had been decimated by the chemotherapy and needed time to recover). However, we managed to agree on a date in November. I would be in hospital for a week and that would be the end of my treatment.

The November date arrived and I was looking forward to this last step in the treatment process. I was feeling well, had been running daily and had regained much of my fitness and was back to my normal weight (65–66 kilograms). A good weight for a distance runner.

The day for the surgery arrived and there I was once again presenting myself at the hospital for admission. I was familiar with the routine having already been admitted for my cancer removal surgery and for day surgery on two occasions. I was scheduled for surgery at 11.30 am, which seemed to arrive quickly and so I was soon being taken to the theatre area. Having arrived, there was the usual routine of being questioned by a nurse to ensure they had the correct person (my name, date of birth, doctor, purpose of the surgery). I was soon in the theatre preparation room chatting to the anaesthetist who I was by now becoming familiar with. The cannula was quickly in place and I was soon drifting off.

After a few hours in the ICU I was transferred to my room in the surgical ward. I had a visit from my surgeon who assured me that the surgery had occurred without any problems. The incision was left open so that the reversal work could be observed to ensure that there were no complications. Hence at this stage I had the stitches inserted but not closed and a surgical dressing covered the incision. This was dressed regularly and checked to ensure that the internal parts that had been resected were okay. This process took place without any problems and after five days the wound was closed.

I felt a great sense of relief that the final step had been undertaken. I had been advised that my system would take time to again function normally. It could be some weeks for it to settle down and may take one to two years for it to be working completely normally. During this time I would experience times of difficulty including alternating bouts of diarrhoea and constipation. I felt confident that I could manage this and that it would progressively move to a normal functioning system.

However within a couple of days of returning home I developed abdominal pains and my abdomen became very tight and extended. I was unable to eat and the abdominal pain became progressively more severe and more frequent. I also had long bouts of diarrhoea. As time went on I also experienced nausea and vomiting. During this period Penny was in contact with my surgeon who made a number of suggestions that might help kickstart my system and overcome the problems that I was experiencing. Unfortunately the situation continued to deteriorate and the pain was by now chronic, forcing me to at times lie doubled-up and holding my abdomen.

This situation couldn't continue and I was put back into hospital for observation and tests. A CT scan was taken which revealed that the radiotherapy had damaged a section of my colon. The damage prevented the colon from functioning normally and I was advised that the damage was not reversible. There was no alternative but further surgery to remove the damaged section of the colon.

After a few days at home I was back in hospital and again preparing to have major surgery. The surgery would take place via an incision along the line of the first surgery (just below the sternum down to the pubic area). I would be in hospital for a week to ten days. I recall being wheeled into the theatre area, being asked the same set of questions by a nurse and then being greeted by the anaesthetist. She was sorry to see me again so soon after the reversal surgery. Although I wasn't that happy about being back in hospital either, the abdominal pain had been so bad that I wanted to have this surgery and to have the damaged section of my colon removed so that I could again move on.

I woke in the ICU and was visited by the surgeon who said the surgery had enabled the removal of the damaged section of colon without any problems. However, removal of the damaged section had meant that there was now no place to attach the remaining colon. This meant that I would have a stoma and require a colostomy and it would be permanent. I had always looked upon the ileostomy as a temporary measure and therefore had no difficulty in coping with it (in fact I was happy to joke about it). However I was now faced with having a permanent device fashioned using a part of my large intestine. Strangely I accepted this without any difficulty. I was free of the pain and discomfort and I was ready to move on, learn how to use this colostomy (as I had done with the ileostomy), get strong, go home and live my cancer-free life.

Unfortunately, it wasn't going to be that simple. Within a short time I became increasingly unwell. My heart rate increased dramatically, likewise my blood pressure and temperature. I recall feeling increasingly drowsy and starting to drift in and out of a state of not being conscious of what was happening to me. There had been a leakage of waste material into my body cavity and I had septicaemia (the presence of disease-causing bacteria). The wheels had now really fallen off and the doctors were very concerned.

Septicaemia – also known as sepsis or blood poisoning – accounts for almost as many deaths each year as heart attacks. Without quick treatment it clearly can be fatal. It is a whole-of-body infection and is usually caused by an infection in one part of the body, such as a wound, that quickly spreads via the bloodstream. Left untreated it can cause dysfunction and failure of body organs leading to respiratory, heart or kidney failure (sometimes several organs are involved). Treatment is usually provided in an intensive care unit, is challenging and requires a high level of experience by nursing and medical staff.

The human body is host to a range of bacteria. For example, bacteria is found in places like the mouth and the bowel. If these bacteria get into the blood stream they can cause disease, particularly if the person is unwell or has an immune system that isn't strong enough to control the invading organism. Having good health is a very good defence against septicaemia. Without quick treatment the bacteria can cause serious complications, including inflammation of organs (heart lining, membrane enclosing the heart, brain or spinal cord), bone or joint infection, organ failure and, as indicated above, death.

I was thus quickly scheduled for more surgery to try and fix the problem. On this occasion the surgery was not optional but was needed to save my life. Penny was advised by some of the doctors that I would be unlikely to survive. My surgeon was apparently a little more optimistic indicating that: 'I would be fighting for my life'. I was unaware of the gravity of the situation as by now I was too ill to be conscious of what was taking place. I was taken to the theatre late in the afternoon. Penny was extremely concerned and would have to wait several hours to find out the outcome. She was invited to wait at the home of close friends, Helen and Keith. This was a long and difficult wait given what she had been told about the seriousness of my condition and about the possibility of survival. Late that evening my surgeon telephoned her to say that the surgery had been completed and had gone as well as could be expected. He indicated that my vital signs had remained stable throughout the surgery. The next 48 hours were apparently critical to my survival but there was now nothing else to do but wait, hope and pray. An update on my condition had been sent by text message to all my close friends and so I am sure there was lots of hoping and praying.

The next thing I remember is waking from the surgery to see a large number of people gathered around my bed, including my surgeon. There were some smiles and a look of relief on several of the faces. I found that I couldn't talk because I had some kind of device in my mouth and throat (an endotracheal tube). A quick look around and I could see that I was once again in the ICU. Penny emerged and after a short time the doctors and nurses left us alone. Penny held my hand and smiled and then said that my children were here and would be pleased to see me awake. I couldn't understand what she meant. Some of my children lived in another city. I suddenly had lots of questions but couldn't speak. A pen and paper were found and so began a series of questions (written with a very shaky hand) and answers.

I had been sedated for four days in order to facilitate my survival. My family had been summoned because there was considerable doubt that I would survive. There had been many very concerned family members, friends and medical staff hovering around in the past four days hoping that I would survive. I was oblivious to this having had a nice four-day rest. Penny had apparently had a very difficult time, particularly during those first critical 48 hours.

The ICU became my home for the next two weeks while the medical staff worked hard to get me to a point where I could be moved into a normal ward. Those two weeks involved some good days and some bad days. I was unable to move, even the smallest amount, without the assistance of two nurses. I found out that I had pneumonia and so needed some vigorous physiotherapy each day. I hated the physiotherapy even though I knew that it was essential. Each day I had to get out of bed and go through a routine with the physiotherapist, culminating in a short walk. I had to hold onto a walker with wheels while the physiotherapist on one side and a nurse on the other assisted me with balance and then to move forward. An oxygen bottle was attached to the front of the walker so that I could have my oxygen fix during the walk. Getting in and out of bed was a major exercise because of all the leads and tubes attached to me and the several bags that were also draining fluids and liquids from my body. The process was slow and required me to stand holding on to the bed, which was not easy and not what I wanted. At the end of each of these sessions I was exhausted. All I wanted to do was lie down and sleep.

Showering involved a similar process, which involved me sitting down with a nurse doing all the work. After my shower, which was almost as exhausting as the walking (even though I just sat there), the nurses usually made me sit for a while before they allowed me to return to bed. I could scratch my nose unassisted, but most other things required a considerable amount of organisation and assistance.

My daily routine involved an X-ray of my chest (taken while I was sat upright in bed with the help of two nurses), several blood tests, lots of visits from doctors, an electrocardiograph (ECG), constant checking by the ICU staff, some medication and of course the interaction with the physiotherapist. I needed help with my breathing and so had an oxygen mask, with which I developed a love-hate relationship: it clearly helped with my oxygen intake, which was measured regularly, but I found it annoying at times. I think my state of health was such that little things often irritated or frustrated me and the oxygen mask was one of the irritants. Twice a day the mask was swapped for a different mask, which contained medication for me to inhale to assist my breathing.

I had an A-line (arterial line) in my left arm so that the medical staff could quickly and easily extract blood for testing. An A-line is used when frequent blood drawing is required and involves insertion of a catheter into an artery, usually in the arm or wrist (often the radial artery). My lower left arm and wrist was bandaged with a rigid board to minimise disturbance of the A-line. A disturbance could cause a bleed, which only happened to me once. The nurses used the A-line to extract blood samples regularly.

I also had a catheter inserted into a vein in the right side of my neck. It was taped and stitched in place. It was used for the administration of medication for quick entry into the blood stream. It gradually became another irritant, as the skin became itchy and I couldn't be shaved in that area which annoyed me. Being shaved made me feel fresh and was something that I sought each day, although I was totally dependent on a nurse or Penny to do the shaving and, like the other daily procedures, left me feeling exhausted.

I also had three tubes inserted into other parts of my body, which were there to collect various substances. The first was in my stomach via my nose and down my throat. It was used to pump unwanted liquid from the stomach, which happened once or twice a day (this prevented me from vomiting). The second tube went to the site of the surgery so that any blood that had accumulated there could be drained into a bag with the help of a small vacuum pump. The third was a catheter into my bladder for draining urine. I also had the stoma draining into another bag. These were the bags that moved with me whenever I moved. Finding a place to put them when I had my daily walk was a challenge. I was literally a 'bag man'.

The day after I regained consciousness I had the breathing device (endotracheal tube) removed from my mouth and throat (known as extubation). The ICU specialist undertook the removal with the usual command of 'take a deep breath'. A quick pull removed it and

I was free of a considerable amount of discomfort. Unfortunately a small piece of my upper lip had become attached to the device and was removed with the device. I was left with a sore lip and a sore throat. After an examination of my mouth and throat I was informed that I had thrush. This involved ongoing oral medication, which had a very unpleasant taste. However, I could at last talk, even if only very softly at first. At this time I was also taken off morphine. On the one hand this was good because the morphine made me feel drowsy (I would at times doze off for a couple of minutes while talking). On the other hand I did have some pain and it would need to be managed in another way. This was also a challenge for me as I was keen to succeed in managing pain without the need for a pain-killing medication.

I was of course being fed intravenously. The saline drip was with me constantly and kept me hydrated. However, my 'food' came twice a day via the drip line in the form of a large black bag. I wasn't offered a menu and there was no choice of flavours. It was to be some time before I would have any food via my mouth. However the black bags kept me from completely fading away.

When in bed, which was most of the time, I was only able to lie on my back. This did present some problems with soreness of the skin particularly in the backside region. I was fortunate to be given frequent massages of those areas with body creams, which I greatly appreciated. Lying on my back also caused the heels of my feet to become very sore and painful. Penny spent lots of time massaging them, which was also a great relief. This was to be an ongoing problem for me during the entire period of my time in hospital.

After a few days Penny arrived one morning, with a large bundle of mail (cards and letters). She suggested that I might be well enough to start reading them. I opened two and read them. Pondering carefully on the wonderful words they contained I announced that I didn't have the strength to continue and asked Penny if she would read them to me. She readily did so and progressively worked her way through about half the bundle. Many messages had also been sent via emails, text and telephone to Penny, which she passed along each day. Flowers had also arrived on an almost daily basis.

As Penny read to me the tears started to roll down my face and I began to cry uncontrollably. This lasted for some time and I had an overwhelming feeling of being loved and cared about by many people. I knew that many people were concerned about my health and were sending up lots of positive thoughts and prayers for my recovery. However, at that moment I was overcome and humbled by the expressions of care in the cards, letters and messages. I said to Penny that I had a very deep realisation about the importance of friends, about what their expressions of care meant and that I need to value friendships more than I had in the past. I decided that I would tell my friends and family how important they are to me and how much I love them. This was something that I was to start doing from that moment. Interestingly, as I did it with those who visited me it seemed to almost immediately deepen the friendship. I think that it had the biggest impact on many of my male friends who felt free to express a sense of closeness in different ways. I received many hugs and kisses during my stay in hospital and this closeness has continued post hospital. This has clearly been a positive outcome from my illness: I felt free to be who I really am in my relationship with friends and family.

In addition to receiving mail, flowers and special food I had a continuing stream of visitors, including many of my running friends. They of course brought news of other runners, of club activities and their latest run and any injuries. This was wonderful and somehow connected me instantly with the running community. I was able to visualise myself still participating in the regular events. On one occasion a long-time running friend, Graham, made one of his regular visits and presented me with a photograph of myself running in my last marathon. This photograph became very important to me as a symbol of what might be possible. It was attached to the wall in my room and became the subject of discussion with nurses, doctors and allied health staff. They were all interested in the story behind the photograph and were generally surprised when I told them that the photograph was taken at about the 34-kilometre mark in a marathon and that I hadn't retired from marathon running. I could see from their facial expressions that they thought I was extremely unrealistic (possibly delusional), given my condition; I imagined them thinking 'he can't even walk without help, so how could he run a marathon?'. But I had a different vision. I was positive I would one day run again. I had already made one comeback and, although this time it would be much harder, I felt that, in time, I could do it again.

**Author at the 34-kilometre mark and in
the hardest part of the marathon**

About part-way through my time in the ICU my nurse advised me that it had been decided to remove the stomach tube and that she would do so immediately. She indicated that patients sometimes experience nausea and vomit when these tubes are removed. Hence I was waterproofed in case I should throw up. She gave the usual command to take a deep breath and then the pulling started. It seemed to go on and on. The tube was much longer than I imagined it to be. It was great to have it out and without any vomiting. The side of my nostril was sore from the tube and I had found the tape that stuck the tube to my nose to be annoying as it frequently came loose. Another tube had been removed.

One day, when I had been in the ICU for two weeks, I heard a discussion amongst senior members of the hospital medical staff about me. Clearly, some of the staff members thought I was ready to be moved out of the ICU, while others thought that I still needed a high level of care. I had personally become a little attached to the security offered by the ICU, but could see that I did need to progress in my recovery – of course, I wasn't consulted on this matter. It was apparent that the hospital wished to empty the ICU for Christmas, which was fast approaching. In the end a compromise was reached; I would be moved but would take an ICU nurse with me for additional care.

The move took place quickly and I was relocated into a room close to the nurse's station in the ward adjoining the ICU. However, before moving me I had to be relieved of my connection to the ICU machinery, which had been monitoring my vital signs constantly for two weeks. I was pleased to be free of these leads and tubes. I also had the patches removed from my body that had connected me to the ECG machine each day. The other attachment to go was the A-line in my left arm. The wires and patches were easily removed but the A-line involved a little more work in removing the catheter from the artery and applying pressure and then a dressing to stop the bleeding. With these matters attended to I was wheeled off to my new room along with my remaining bags and the oxygen.

The new room was different and certainly not large, but was bright and had much less movement than the ICU. I would now need to ring the bell for a nurse, although I would still have frequent attention because of the extra nursing care. I had for several days questioned the continuing need for the tube in my neck, as it hadn't been used for medication recently. While in the ICU I was not able to make any progress on this matter, but now that I was out I renewed my push to have it removed. This took place within two days of moving to the ward. Another tube was gone and this meant that I could now have a complete shave, which, psychologically, was important to me.

With Christmas only two days away it was decided to move me even closer to the nurses' station and so I was moved up the hall into a similar but slightly larger room. Christmas morning came and I was visited by friends Bette, Brian, Helen and Brendan, who brought good wishes and a song they sang to the accompaniment of a ukulele. It was great to see them, although I didn't feel very merry and wasn't particularly responsive.

My family came a little later on Christmas morning for a 'party' and some presents. I was able to sit in a chair amongst the group. They had brought along some drinks and some nibbles. I was still being fed via the drip line but could drink. Although no bubbly this year for me, I managed a very small sip of carbonated drink. We all made the best of the situation. The children were cheerful, which was nice, but all I wanted to do was climb back into bed.

Later in the morning our close friend, Neale, who was the minister from our church, visited us. He had prepared a special brief Christmas liturgy for us. We shared that with him, which was wonderful although I wasn't feeling particularly well on Christmas Day. Neale was aware of the state of my health and my attitude to the journey that I was on and had crafted special words with great care and love. I have a copy of what Neale wrote and have read the words a number of times over the last few years. I always feel a little bit emotional when I read them and appreciate just how appropriate they were at that time and how much thought Neale had put into crafting them. The last part, which I have included below, was about the journey, including the difficulties, frustrations and the unexpected.

The Journey Onwards

There will be no camels
We are going to have to walk
At least for some of the way.

And we won't arrive there a few hours before everyone else.
It will be weeks perhaps …
Or months.

We are not in a hurry,
Although we may be frustrated.

We will take the time to heal,
To talk
To rest
And walk a little further each day.

We will talk of travels we will undertake
We are curious people
And we want to learn.

We will look in some of the wrong places.
We admit that,
Because wise men, intellectuals, strong women
Call us what you will –
We are not infallible.

We expect a new power
To emerge from the side of the old one.
We expect the destination we seek
To resemble what our common sense deduces.
We suspect we know the path
Even if it is as yet untraveled.

But when we think we arrive,
God has been there before us.

But that is the trouble with God.
He does not leave you as you came.
He sends you back
Stripped of your presumptions
Making for home by another way.

Penny as usual stayed with me all day. I commented that I was not feeling as well as I had been the previous day or so.

The following day my temperature rose dramatically above the normal range. This started a period of abnormal temperatures. I was so hot that cold towels were applied to my body to assist in keeping me cool. Penny was kept busy wetting the towels and replacing them as they dried. It was decided that I would have a CT scan to see if a cause could be identified. As it was Boxing Day staff had to be summoned to perform the scan. The results showed that I had a number of pockets of infection in my body that could not be reached and treated by the antibiotics. Hence I would need to have tubes inserted to each of these locations in order to drain the infected material.

The following day the CT staff were back, together with a radiologist to start the job of inserting the tubes. By this time I was oscillating between being extremely cold and boiling hot. I was wheeled in to the CT room and lifted onto the base. The CT was used to locate each area where a tube needed to be inserted. It was decided that the first tube should be inserted into my abdomen to a large pocket of infected material. This was done with a local anaesthetic and a small incision followed by the insertion of a wire to the location of the infection. A tube was then inserted over the wire, which was withdrawn. It felt as though the process was taking a very long time. This was probably because I was feeling unwell and I was by now extremely cold. It in fact took about an hour.

As soon as the insertion was completed a syringe was used to extract a sample of the material for analysis. At this point the room was filled with the most pungent and unpleasant smell (which Penny, who was waiting outside with two doors between us, smelt). The radiologist commented that it was better out than in. I was taken back to my room and packed with hot blankets to warm me up. The process of inserting tubes was repeated over the next few days until I had tubes inserted to all infected areas. I felt a bit like a porcupine. Each of the tubes had a bag attached to collect the material being drained.

Within a few days my temperature settled down to be largely within the normal range, only occasionally moving above the top of normal. I again started to feel a little better and felt that I must now surely be on my way to recovery.

My surgeon had decided that it was time to remove the catheter into my bladder and that it was also time for me to start eating. After a few weeks of being fed intravenously twice a day from a black bag of 'food' I would now have to try to eat normally.

I had the catheter removed soon after the decision. It involved the usual direction to take a deep breath and then, with a quick pull, it was gone. Starting to eat again was a little more complicated and problematic. Because I had not eaten for such a long time my body had responded by switching off my appetite. This is part of the body's defence mechanism to keep you alive in a situation where you may be stranded without food. I also had problems swallowing because of what had happened to the inside of my throat. Another problem was that my stomach had become accustomed to not having food in it and so had contracted a little.

My doctor had emphasised that once the bags were taken away I would need to ensure that I ate a sufficient amount of food. I couldn't afford to lose any more weight and eating normally was important to my recovery. To help with my reintroduction to food I had a discussion with the hospital dietitian. She suggested types of food that would be best and arranged for a supply of high-energy drinks. The dietitian also suggested that Penny might be able to cook some food that might be easier for me to eat and that would contain a range of ingredients that would promote weight gain. Because Penny spent so much time at the hospital cooking food for me was not possible. She mentioned this to two of our friends, Trish and David, who immediately said they would cook some food and also devise a roster of other friends to bring dinner each night. This was quickly in place and dinner arrived each evening about 5 pm for the remainder of my stay in hospital. There was dinner not only for me but also Penny. This was an incredible act of love and support by Trish, Bette, Joan, and two Helens. I had great difficulty swallowing and could only eat small amounts. This was taken into consideration and the food that arrived was designed to be swallowed easily and contained wonderful life sustaining ingredients.

Although I'd now overcome my temperature problem, unfortunately this wasn't to be my last problem as I had one more major drama to go through. My daily blood tests were monitoring progress in a number of key areas of the functioning of my body. The results had been showing a progressive improvement in all areas and most readings were by now either normal or close to normal except for one important measure, which had started to move into the abnormal range. This reading was a measure of my bilirubin, which monitors liver function (including acting as an indicator of liver disorders). The reading was progressively rising. While there is no 'normal' reading because bilirubin is an excretion product, the reading should be in the range of about 5 to 20. My reading was well above 20 and so my medical team once again became very concerned.

I was sent for a range of tests and scans to see if there was a problem with any other part of my body which could be having an adverse impact on my liver. For example, it was thought that there might be gallstones, which can have this effect on the liver. All the tests were clear and by now I was starting to show the effects of a malfunctioning liver. I was turning yellow and I had gained weight as a result of the fluid that was gathering in my body. I was not feeling particularly comfortable and my health once again took a nosedive. The doctors tried a number of things to try to reverse the increasing level of bilirubin, including blood transfusions. Nothing worked and each day the reading climbed higher. It was by now over 200.

While many doctors within and outside the hospital had been consulted it was decided to seek the opinion of another gastroenterologist. A visit from this new gastroenterologist occurred soon after the decision was made. He arrived one evening looking a little like the mad professor and after a brief chat and physical examination he said that in his opinion the antibiotic that I was receiving was poisoning my liver. He had read in the medical literature a report on that particular antibiotic which reported that in a very small number of instances it had poisoned the liver of the recipient. In his opinion I should be taken off the antibiotic and he stated he would recommend this to my surgeon. I had been receiving antibiotics since the surgery and they had been changed and doses adjusted from time to time. Given the level of infection in my body antibiotic treatment had been deemed essential.

Later that evening a nurse came to my room and said that my doctor had telephoned to say that I was to receive no further doses of the antibiotic and I was also to be taken off all other medication and the saline drip was also to be removed.

I was not sorry to have the drip removed but to withdraw all medication involved some risk that infections might re-emerge. I still had several tubes in my body that continued to drain infected material. As I recall there was a collective deep breath taken that night. While my next blood test showed no reduction in my bilirubin reading it had at least risen no further. We were also waiting to see if my temperature would again rise. There were a couple of slightly higher temperature readings but they were at the high end of the normal range, which was okay. Over the next 12 hours there were many crossed fingers all hoping that my temperature would stay in the normal range and my liver functioning would improve. The next blood test was going to be very important. The young nurse arrived as usual about 7 am with the trolley containing all the equipment for taking blood. She was very efficient at extracting blood and I liked her as she was cheerful and we always talked about her current cycling activities and my (past) running activities.

A few hours later the results were in and a nurse came to say that the bilirubin reading had dropped a little. There were smiles and a huge sigh of relief, particularly as my temperature had remained in the normal range. On each successive day the reading dropped, the yellow skin gradually returned to a normal colour and the excess fluid started to disappear.

My physiotherapy treatment had continued on a daily basis, even during my ups and downs. At times it was difficult and frustrating for me as I had little energy and strength and so doing exercises (even though they were very basic) was a major challenge. I had been fit and had lots of energy before this journey began, and so my current condition continued to be a source of frustration. However I wanted to get back some of the lost muscle tissue and so persisted. At times I did more than was required, pushing myself to do that little bit extra. I recall collapsing into bed on many occasions after my walk (with the aid of a walker on wheels) and my exercise routine. I would be exhausted, tired and depleted. I sometimes felt angry that I couldn't do what I regarded as simple exercises without great difficulty.

During much of my stay in hospital Penny slept by my bedside at night. This was a wonderful act of love on her part and a great support for me. She started sleeping at the hospital after I came out of the ICU and continued until the liver problem was resolved and I was clearly much improved. She responded many times to assist me during the night. She was able to respond immediately whereas the night nurses sometimes took several minutes to reach my room. Each morning she would assist me with breakfast (once I started eating) and then go home and shower, attend to a few domestic matters and quickly return to the hospital. There were always lots of text messages and emails to respond to. Text message bulletins were sent out to various groups to update on my condition. While it was wonderful to have Penny at the hospital most of the day and night I did feel a little guilty about this. However I also knew that it was where she wanted to be, such was the depth of her love and concern for me. We discussed this a number of times and agreed that experiencing what I had experienced without support would be extremely difficult. I often thought about people who might be in the same state of health as me but who had no support. I couldn't imagine how difficult this would be for someone in that position.

Now that I was improving daily it was suggested that Penny might like to take me home for a few hours as a way of progressively reintroducing me back to normal living. However, before doing this it was decided that most of my tubes, which were draining infected material, could come out because the collection bags were empty. The removal process involved collapsing the inserted end of the tube by releasing a fine string and then pulling the tube quickly (on the command of 'take a deep breath'). They all came out easily except for one that refused to budge and every attempt to remove it resulted in pain for me. They persisted and after much consultation and what seemed like a very long time the tube relented and came out. I was left with one tube in place in my back, which was still draining material from a pocket of infection located just above my left kidney.

I was now ready go home for a visit. The plan was for me to leave hospital in the afternoon and stay out for a couple of hours before returning at about 5 pm. With some assistance I made it to the front entrance of the hospital and then into our car. It was a very hot summer day, which I particularly noticed having come from an air-conditioned hospital. The short drive home felt very strange. It was as though I was in some kind of alien environment, unfamiliar and not exactly real. We were quickly home and the car came to a stop in the garage under the house. To get to the front door I had to climb a flight of stairs to the first floor. As I was unable to walk without assistance this was not an easy climb and required several pauses and lots of assistance from Penny (just as well I was a lightweight).

We repeated the process of having a short home visit several times. The first couple of times I felt a little uneasy about being away from the hospital. It was hard to explain but I had clearly become accustomed to the routine, support and the security that the hospital provided. Hence, at around 4 pm I would start to suggest that it might be time to think about getting back to the hospital.

Then came the next step when my surgeon suggested that I go home late afternoon and stay overnight, returning after breakfast the following morning. Again this made me feel a little insecure but was probably much more effective than going 'cold turkey'. I had been very ill and had several major setbacks, so there was probably a subconscious fear that if a further problem occurred we couldn't respond to it as quickly at home.

Although I hadn't been sleeping very well in hospital, I found that my first night home involved little sleep. I had become accustomed to sleeping on my back in hospital and I had a special mattress, which constantly moved air around to create the effect of movement in the bed. Lying awake on what felt like a much harder surface (even though we have a very comfortable bed) was not a restful night. I also had sore heals and pains in my legs which meant that I had to sit on the edge of the bed several times during the night. This would be a problem for me for several months. This was a difficult time for Penny and me, as I needed a considerable amount of assistance to do even the simplest of tasks.

After eight weeks in hospital I was finally told that it was time to leave. Following breakfast one morning my room was packed up and I said goodbye to many nurses and doctors that had become a part of my life during a very difficult period. They were pleased to see me depart and it was clear that some who had seen me at some of my low points were surprised that I had made it. We were assisted to the front door and into the car. This time it was the real thing and not a trial at being home.

I went home weighing 52 kilograms, looking like someone who had just been released from a labour camp and unable to do very much without assistance. Those once strong muscled running legs were now thin sticks, which could not function like they had for so many years. I needed assistance to get to the car but I had with me the photograph of myself competing in my last marathon. This photograph went straight onto the wall of our study when I arrived home. However, I now had to face the question of how I would get my legs back to their former shape and strength. Clearly this would be a major undertaking, but essential if I was to get back to running again – which I had dreamed of so often while in intensive care. I would first have to learn to walk again, given that I could only manage a few steps unaided. I also had to regain the weight I had lost and this would require a return of appetite. This was to be a challenge given that I found eating more than a few mouthfuls difficult and I had lost my sense of taste. Hence walking, exercise and eating programs were designed and I started the slow process of rehabilitation.

Chapter 6

Life on the Outside

*In the infinity of life where I am, all is perfect, whole
and complete. I recognize my body as a good friend.
Each cell in my body has Divine Intelligence. I listen
to what it tells me, and know that its advice is valid. I
am always safe, and Divinely protected and guided. I
choose to be healthy and free. All is well in my world.*

You Can Heal Your Life. Louise L Hay

It was now time for me to enter an entirely new phase in my life. I
was now home and needed to learn to live normally again. However,
the exercises were difficult, the walking very tiring and the eating
a challenge. I guess I wanted quick results but clearly it was going
to take time and a considerable amount of effort and commitment.
I felt a level of frustration because of the slow progress and the
limitations on what I could do. After all, I had exercised and run
each day for many years and loved food. The exercises and walking
were done until exhaustion (which at first came very quickly and
usually resulted in me collapsing onto a bed, often sleeping for a long
period of time). Penny and friends cooked wonderful and enticing
food, which made me feel that I needed to work hard at regaining

my appetite and love for food. The hospital dietitian told me that it would take six or more months for me to regain the lost weight. In fact this turned out to be the easiest task to master and I regained my weight and almost had my full sense of taste back within three months.

I quickly established a routine of walking each day. At first I only managed very short walks and had lots of trouble with my breathing. This was another frustration for me, as, thanks to my running, I had never had any problems with breathing. I had always been a good hill runner (which had tested my lungs) and had won many mountain-running championships in my age group, including an Australian championship in 2005. I now also walked differently. My left leg swung out much like someone who had suffered a stroke. One of my fitness advisers had cautioned me to be careful walking and especially if I started to run as my brain would require a bit of reprogramming on how to do simple tasks like stepping over an obstacle or up guttering onto a footpath. The reprogramming would occur in the doing but I had to be careful or my legs may not get the signal from my brain and so I could easily fall. I did stumble lots of times and I must have looked rather awkward with my swinging left leg but I persisted and thankfully I managed to avoid falling.

By the end of six months I was again walking for two hours a day and pushing myself so that I was working my lungs as hard as possible, forcing my cardiovascular system to also work hard. I was by this time also able to walk with a fairly normal gait and had certainly eliminated the left leg kick. I had also gained a considerable amount of fitness through the walking, exercises, stretches and sessions on a stationary bike.

The stationary bike was recommended by a trainer as a very good way to increase my fitness and strength. My balance was not particularly good and on the first session on the bike the bike and I fell over and I ended up on the floor with the bike on top of me. My stationary bike sessions did improve and although I found indoor cycling boring it did help improve my fitness.

In the exercise department I particularly concentrated on leg strengthening exercises. As time went by I also started to do some light upper-body weights to regain strength in that part of my body. This was all done with considerable difficulty and often led to exhaustion. Not surprisingly, I again became frustrated because the progress in regaining my fitness was so difficult and slow.

I had one particular ongoing frustration which was similar to a problem that I had experienced after the initial surgery to remove the cancer. This was an anal discharge that had commenced while I was in hospital. It caused lots of discomfort and frustration. The volume of the discharge was greater than on the previous occasion and often contained blood. I was forced to use pads day and night, which were useful but a constant reminder that I wasn't yet fully healed. My surgeon indicated that the discharge would eventually stop but he could not predict how long this would take. I would just have to be patient. After several months I noticed that there was almost no discharge at night and then gradually it slowed during the day. Then one day it was gone.

It was a bit like a miracle; a wonderful feeling not having to deal with this anymore or the constant reminder that all was not well. It is difficult to describe the difference this change made to my wellbeing. Having it was an ever-present reminder of my health problems but now I suddenly felt healthy. This was an incredible boost to my mental health. In retrospect I should have tried harder to not allow it to annoy me so much and allow it to make me feel angry at times.

During each of my periods in hospital and subsequent recovery I received a number of books from friends, often with an accompanying message of encouragement and concern. These books frequently arrived at a time in the process when they were helpful because they contained useful information or were inspirational or provided motivation or were simply a wonderful distraction. I often marvelled at the arrival of these books at such a useful time in my treatment. One of the books to arrive was by Andy Griffiths (*The*

Day My Bum Went Psycho), which coincided with my frustration caused by the discharge problem. It came from close friend Granton with the message: 'This book may be an inspiration to you'. It was both an inspiration and a wonderful distraction during that period.

Some six months after my discharge from hospital, winter again arrived and with it, the ski season. As I indicated earlier, Penny and I would normally go to the snow at this time of year for a week or so skiing. An opportunity to go to the snow arose when accommodation became available at our ski lodge and so, like the previous year, the question arose about the possibility of my body being ready to ski.

This is probably sounding like a repeat of the situation that occurred the previous year. However, the difference is that in between the two ski seasons I had survived a very difficult period involving two months in hospital, and I had emerged unable to do even the most basic tasks unaided – including walking. While I had made significant progress since leaving hospital I still had not regained my normal strength and my balance was not perfect. After a very short discussion Penny and I decided (as we had done the previous year) that we would go and if I couldn't ski then we would treat the time at the snow like a holiday.

Following breakfast at the lodge on the first morning we pulled on the ski gear, grabbed the skis and jumped into the bus to take us down the hill to the bottom of the ski runs. It was in fact something of an effort carrying the skis and walking steadily in the ski boots (not easy at the best of times). After a few deep breaths the lift tickets were purchased and we were on the chairlift to the top of the mountain. There was a touch of déjà vu about this. Hadn't I done this last year? I was very familiar with the ski runs and was aware that the first part of the run involved a steep but short slope requiring a few turns.

We were as usual skiing with some friends and at the top of this slope I paused to let the others go first and to do some self-talk. How would these legs, which were only a few months ago very thin and weak, respond to the short sharp turns that were necessary to navigate the slope? There was no time to think any more as the others were waiting at the bottom of the slope. I pointed the skis down the slope and launched myself. Three turns later and I was at the bottom with the others and still upright. The legs and the brain had responded and so I was able to ski that day and two more days with very few difficulties.

Being a reasonable skier I managed to avoid all but about three spills. Falling over did no physical damage but created a new problem for me. Regaining an upright position proved to be impossible. My legs were strong enough to ski but not to push my body upwards. This caused some amusement for the group and there was some talk about leaving me prostrate in the snow. I was however pulled to my feet on each occasion. I collapsed into bed each night satisfied but somewhat exhausted. Being able to ski was a great boost to my confidence and another marker that I was on track with my rehabilitation.

Skiing was an important activity for me for a number of reasons. Being in the mountain environment was always a wonderful experience and gliding along on skis was a great feeling. However I particularly valued the experience because it required my undivided attention. I had to be completely in the moment. It's one of the few things that I do that requires me to be fully in the now. As noted earlier, to be otherwise would lead to disaster. Eckhart Tolle has written extensively about being in the now (e.g. *The Power of Now*), which he describes as accepting the present moment unconditionally and without reservation. This is what skiing does for me without any effort. Being in the now at other times can be difficult as the mind tends to dwell in the past or the future even though the only thing that is real is the now. I believe that this is something that I need to continue to work on as it's important for my ongoing personal growth (I will return to this is a later part of this book).

About a month later, after my morning walk, I decided that I needed to move on from the long daily walks and try running for a short distance. The next morning I put on my running gear, did some stretches and headed out the door for a run. This was something I had done hundreds of times before, but this time it felt very strange. I ran very slowly for a little over 1.5 kilometres and then turned and retraced my steps. It was not easy like my running used to be, but it was physically manageable with considerable effort and a lot of concentration. My lungs and legs groaned but I ignored their calls for me to stop and they responded to my urging to keep going. I was disappointed at the level of effort required but I nevertheless felt extremely pleased. I had finished the run gasping for breath and with aching legs, but I had managed to finish it. I ran again on the following day (4 km), and then had a rest for a few days and then I was out there each day running 4 kilometres. It was very difficult and very slow, but more importantly, I was again a runner.

About three weeks later I participated in a cross-country relay, running a 3-kilometre section of the relay for the team. Compared to my previous standard I was oh so very slow, but I was out there again with lots of encouragement from my running friends. It was a two-lap course and I recall vividly the enormous amount of encouragement I received after the first lap.

I slowly increased the distance of my daily run and after a further two months I was running 6 kilometres daily. Some days were good and some days were a real struggle but I was back running and that was very important to me. When I am running I sleep soundly and I enjoy food. Hence being back running helped my rehabilitation in a number of important ways.

Regaining full strength in my legs and getting my lungs to work properly was clearly going to be a long process. Even with daily running and lots of leg exercises and stretching I had difficulty in lifting my body up using my legs. For example I found it impossible to place one foot on a chair and then attempt to pull my other foot onto the chair so that I could retrieve some object from a high shelf. This could only be achieved with a pull up at the same time, which meant I needed to have something to hold and pull against. It was many months before I could undertake this task relatively easily. I had lost my muscle power in my legs, which had been a product of years of running. It was clear that this would take months (even years) to completely regain.

I also had difficulty with my breathing. I couldn't seem to get my lungs to work like they did before my two months in hospital. I found myself gasping for breath at times on my daily runs. This was a new experience for me and a frustration. I had always been able to breathe easily even when pushing my body uphills. In fact I was always a very good hill runner and, as I mentioned previously, I managed to be very competitive in my age group in mountain-running competitions. At times I wondered if my lungs would ever improve and contemplated if the pneumonia had damaged them permanently. However, after a few months, I noticed some improvement, which although small gave me reason to believe that time and exercise would lead to further improvement.

But while my running continued to improve, since leaving hospital I had been having some difficulties with my stoma as a result of it prolapsing. This is one complication that can occur with a colostomy. A prolapse occurs when the colon extends and telescopes outwards through the current stoma. This causes the stoma to grow in length from about 5 to 25 centimetres. The prolapsing action made it difficult for the plate attached to my skin to stay in place and hence I was finding it difficult to keep a bag in place. I was therefore forced to frequently (sometimes daily) replace the plate.

I consulted my surgeon about this a few weeks after leaving hospital. He indicated that I would need further surgery to redo the stoma. While I was keen to have this additional work done as soon as possible he felt that I needed to wait a few months to regain health and strength. He was also concerned that I might have a negative psychological reaction to hospital if I went back too quickly. I didn't think that I would react negatively to a return to hospital (after all I had by now been in hospital several times). However I subsequently found that he was right. I was driving near the hospital not long after my consultation with the surgeon and had a bad reaction. Although I couldn't actually see the hospital I knew it was there and I felt a sense of alarm. This happened several times to me including when I was close to another hospital where I had been administered my chemotherapy. However this feeling and sensation passed and just before Christmas almost 11 months after leaving hospital I was again admitted to have surgery on my stoma.

I was back into very familiar territory and the routine and procedures at the operating theatre were the same. I remained in hospital for five days and this time I was keen to get home. I was not permitted to run for about three weeks, which meant that I had to wait until just before New Year's Day until I could start running again. But by mid-January I had increased my daily run to 7 kilometres and the stoma was now working very well. No more prolapsing.

I still had one further piece of surgery to undergo. The Portacath was still in place and would need to be removed at some point. It had to be flushed every four to five weeks to ensure that it was functioning and ready for use in case I needed further chemotherapy. I was clear in my mind that I would not require further chemotherapy but the oncologist said I would need to wait a little longer and so I had to continue my regular visits to the oncology unit for the flushing. The only positive thing about this was that I was able to catch up with the oncology nurses and let them see the progress I had made. I was still having regular blood tests and the Portacath was also useful for this purpose.

Twenty months after finishing my chemotherapy I was admitted to hospital for day surgery to remove the Portacath. There were no complications with the surgery and my oncologist had indicated that he was of the view that the cancer would not return because of the treatment that I had received. This was fantastic and although I knew that I would need to see my doctors periodically and would require regular blood tests, a periodic colonoscopy and some scans as part of the follow-up process, I felt an immense sense of relief and freedom. It was now time to really get on with life.

Chapter 7

Why Me?

Instead of consciously creating disease, we could be consciously creating health.

Journey into Healing. Deepak Chopra

I indicated in the first part of this book that the pronouncement that I had rectal cancer was a big shock to me because I was so healthy and fit, didn't get sick and therefore had never contemplated having a major health problem. I was almost indestructible. Or so I thought. Hence, when I heard the words: 'You have rectal cancer, it's large and it's been there for some time', I experienced a sense of disbelief. Surely the gastroenterologist was talking about someone else. However the reality of my situation became apparent fairly quickly. I had cancer, it was large and the gastroenterologist had a photograph of it in colour to show me (a copy of which is reproduced in the first chapter of this book).

I have read stories about other people discovering they had cancer or some other disease and asking the question 'why me?'. I have lived a good life. I did no harm to others. I have worked hard to do good works in my community. It seems that for some people the news that they have a major health problem generates feelings of guilt and recrimination ('I must have caused the cancer').

While I never felt guilty I was extremely curious about the question: 'why me?'. In fact it was a question that I returned to examine many times. You might say that it was a question that I couldn't leave alone and to which I needed to find an answer. For me answering this question was complicated by the fact that I felt I had taken care to ensure that I stayed healthy. I had very deliberately for many years done all the things that I believed were necessary to maintain a fit and healthy body: I had run almost every day for 30 years; I had eaten all the right types of food (lots of fruit and vegetables, low fat food, low salt and plenty of fibre); I had never smoked; and I wasn't overweight (possibly even a little thin for my height and age). My friends and work colleagues would tell me that I looked healthy and younger than my age, and in over 20 years I hadn't taken a single day off work with illness. I had a busy and demanding job but I believed that I was very experienced and was thus able to handle tight deadlines and a large workload in a mature non-stressful way. Hence I considered that work-related stress was not a problem for me. Since my diagnosis I have had lots of time to think about these matters and have examined and re-examined these factors and my life style in order to try and understand why I had rectal cancer. Some people might think that I should just be thankful that I've been cured and move on, but I couldn't do that.

Because of my level of fitness I always had lots of energy. I was aware that my daily routine of exercise over a number of years had changed my body composition so that I had maximised the amount of muscle tissue in my body. I was also aware that it was this muscle tissue that gave me the energy to undertake lots of physical activity, including running long distances. I often had people say to me: 'I don't know where you get your energy from'. I knew where it came from and I even felt a little smug and superior that I had so much vitality while others complained of being tired. My ego was clearly very healthy and at times I enjoyed a feeling of superiority because of my high level of fitness and good health (my neurotic pride in action). This image I had of myself was my sense of self that I had come to idealise and worked hard to maintain.

I also had cancer and clearly wasn't indestructible after all. Coming to grips with this was very confronting. I was initially shocked and my pride had also been damaged. How would my ego cope? I needed to know what caused my cancer.

Hence the question of what had caused my cancer was one that I pursued over many months. I pondered about it on many wakeful occasions in the middle of the night while I lay in a hospital bed. For me this wasn't about how unfortunate I was, or how unjust this was, but it was about being very curious to understand the cause. I also didn't blame anyone, including myself (although I did think how different it might have been had I had that colonoscopy much earlier).

I had for some time been reading a wide range of personal development material and had attempted to understand what the authors were saying and how this applied to me. As a result I had some insights and I had made small changes to the way I operated. Having embarked on this journey of personal discovery several years before my diagnosis was useful to me in exploring the question of 'why me?'.

I sometimes struggled to fully understand the relevance of some of this personal development material to me. Changing old ways of doing and being can be difficult, particularly when old ways seemed to have worked and when there is a subconscious resistance to change. I was very fortunate in having someone who had done a considerable amount of personal growth work that could discuss, interpret and challenge me as I grappled with my own personal journey. This was my best friend, my lover and my wife, Penny. She often shared insights with me, encouraged me and challenged me to make changes. Many times she said: 'Tell me how you feel, not what you think'. This is difficult for a person who thinks a lot and has always tried to work things out intellectually.

This exploration had progressively given me some insights, which not only prompted me to make changes but also drove me to undertake further exploration in search of new knowledge and understanding. As a consequence of doing this work I had many thoughts and feelings about my cancer and why I got it. These thoughts led me to examine other material, including writings in the health, medical, philosophy, psychology and spirituality areas. This of course answered some questions, but also generated other questions and gave me more to think about. Let me share some of my findings and thoughts with you.

In the health and medical literature there is clearly evidence that indicates that having a family member who has had cancer increases your risk of having cancer (in Australia in 25 per cent of colorectal cancer cases there is a family history). In my case my mother, at the age of 81 years, was diagnosed with bowel cancer. Hence it would seem that because of my mother's cancer I had one risk factor for cancer. My mother had surgery, recovered and lived on into her 90s without any further sign of cancer.

In my quest to understand my cancer I looked at the question of predisposition in another way. There is a considerable body of evidence that indicates that some of us, because of our genetic make-up, are predisposed or more susceptible to certain illnesses or diseases. In some cases this predisposition could be inherited. However, it seems that even though we may have a predisposition this doesn't necessarily mean that we will end up with the disease or illness we are predisposed towards. In other words we go through life unaware of this, leading a normal healthy life.

It appears that what is required for a disease to develop is the existence of some additional factor or factors. This means that the circumstances or conditions must be right for the illness to occur. This is described by some as a trigger. Hence the question arose for me as to what might have been a trigger for me if I had a predisposition to rectal (or colorectal) cancer.

Attempting to find the answer to this question took me on a

journey – a journey of reading and thinking that lasted several years. It was a journey that did not always move in logical steps and was sometimes coloured by past events and emotions.

I often found myself returning to thinking about my pre-cancer lifestyle – eating well, not smoking, exercising, and having excellent blood pressure, a low resting heart rate, low cholesterol – but still ending up with a serious illness.

I thus kept pursuing this question of why. For me the way forward was often to explore what many others had to say about illness and disease and their prevention and causes.

A number of factors emerged repeatedly as causes or triggers of disease and they include the following:

- Having a close family member with a disease (which I have already mentioned, and more relevant for certain types of diseases including cancer as per my previous discussion).

- Having one or more of what are described particularly in the medical literature as major risk factors. These may include, smoking, excess alcohol, sedentary life style, being overweight, an unhealthy diet, and of course these may vary from disease to disease. What may happen here is that any one or more of these may act as a trigger to some underlying predisposition.

- Dealing with stress and anxiety over a prolonged period (which may come from work, financial matters, marriage break-up, death of a significant person). There is a considerable amount written about the negative impact of prolonged stress, which clearly points to it as a potential trigger for illness.

- Experiencing aloneness, such as living alone, having few social contacts or networks (it seems that friends and family and social activity are very important to wellbeing and health). There is an increasing emphasis on these factors as important in staying healthy and living longer.

- Being unhappy and/or angry (people who are continuously in this state seem to become ill more frequently and die younger). There is a lot written about unhappiness and anger (including causes and negative impacts) in the health and personal development literature.

Some of these issues are regularly reported in the media and hence there is a reasonable level of community awareness of them. Often the reporting relates to specific findings of research on an individual disease. For example, for many years there has been a concerted effort to inform the public about the risk factors associated with heart disease, updated periodically following the release of new information about issues such as smoking, poor eating habits, lack of exercise and excessive drinking of alcohol. There has also been much written in the media about the possible consequences of having particular genes, again with a focus on the findings of research and medical practice relating to how this can lead to a particular disease (e.g. heart disease, types of cancer). We have also been made aware of many of these factors because of the work of organisations and bodies that promote awareness of particular diseases and attempt to advocate to the community to reduce their risk by changing their habits and lifestyles. The National Heart Foundation and Bowel Cancer Australia are good examples of Australian organisations that have undertaken this role for a long period of time.

In more recent years there has been a considerable amount of publicity given to breast cancer, as well as a program aimed at increasing the rate of testing for colorectal cancer in people 50 years of age or over. While some of the other factors listed above aren't reported as comprehensively in the popular press (or as often), they are nevertheless reported periodically and are certainly written about in some detail in other literature. The stories about health problems of famous people possibly reach the greatest number of people.

However I suspect that these stories are mainly of general interest to readers rather than effecting change in behaviour such as occurs with a well-developed long-term program (e.g. the program to reduce the rate of smoking).

However, awareness does not necessarily lead us to take action on advice that would likely reduce or eliminate risk. Advice often incorporates a suggestion about the importance of regular checks, involving a doctor or participation in some screening activity. In my case I had periodically undertaken full health assessments that concluded that I was a wonderful example of a healthy person – not only for my age but also more generally. I had participated in a bowel-screening program some 15 years prior to my cancer diagnosis but had considered that my overall level of health and fitness, combined with my lifestyle, made bowel cancer almost impossible. Clearly I was very wrong.

Following my diagnosis I was advised to talk to my children about colorectal cancer and to impress upon them that they need to have a colonoscopy around the age of 40 years. Had I done this on reaching the age of 40, or as soon as my mother was diagnosed with cancer, I would most probably not be writing about having rectal cancer. Unfortunately, my mother was not advised to tell me to be tested and it simply didn't occur to me (probably because I felt so healthy and was at the time concerned about my mother's recovery). As I indicated previously it's easy to remove polyps (small pieces of bulging tissue) during a colonoscopy, which, if left, sometimes result in rectal or bowel cancer.

The discovery of my cancer led many of my friends and work colleagues to have a colonoscopy and as a result several of them had polyps removed without any further problems. I am very pleased that my diagnosis was instrumental in others acting to take care of their health. These were all educated and well-informed people, but it took the shock of an event such as my cancer diagnosis to propel them into action to be tested.

If some of the causal factors are promoted and written about frequently in the media, and yet are disregarded, then other factors that don't have the same level of media attention, or that may seem a little more remote or unlikely to be relevant, are possibly much more easily ignored. These factors possibly include loneliness (living alone, few or no friends and networks), a major stressful event and being continually unhappy and/or angry. As I mentioned previously these matters have been reported in a number of ways in recent years but are possibly easy to ignore or in some cases difficult if not impossible to change (e.g. changing living circumstances, increasing the number of friends).

In my quest to understand why I got cancer I have examined each of the factors that I listed above. I've already commented on my possible predisposition to bowel cancer because my mother had bowel cancer. I also investigated the causes of death of other family members and could find no record that there were others with bowel cancer. In my view a predisposition based on one family member (who was 81 when diagnosed) was not the reason why I developed cancer. Clearly I should have had a colonoscopy when my mother was diagnosed.

Let me now comment on the other factors progressively working towards the one that I think may have been a trigger for me. Regarding the elimination of health risk factors I believe that I scored highly as someone with a low number of the common risk factors. For the sake of completeness in this analysis I will repeat briefly what I have already stated about my lifestyle. At the time of my diagnosis: I had never smoked; I exercised daily; and I ate lots of vegetables and fruit and foods that were low in fat, salt and sugar. I was at that time (and still am) very interested in cooking and liked exploring recipes and options for cooking healthy food. I didn't drink alcohol excessively but I did drink alcohol regularly (those who argue for a total alcohol abstinence approach to health may conclude that this was a negative for me). I have never had a problem with excess weight – it has always been towards the lower end of the normal range for my age and height and has been very stable all my life (except when doing hard marathon training when it always went down a little). My assessment of this group is to dismiss them as not being relevant as a cause for my cancer.

On the matter of being alone, or having few or no networks of friends and family, I think it would be clear from what I've said earlier that this is unlikely to be a factor in my case – there are so many wonderful people that I enjoy being with, and who have been very supportive throughout this journey. These include my loving and supportive family and my wonderful wife, with whom I get to share many great experiences, as well as my friends through my many interests (including my running).

With regard to stress as a factor in causing my cancer I did comment earlier that I believe that even though I worked in a job with lots of pressure I was not stressed by the pressure that came with the job. I have looked at this area of my life a number of times and each time I have concluded that I was not stressed by my work. There was certainly an adrenaline rush at times, but not ongoing stress of the type that made me dread work. On the contrary, I enjoyed my work and looked forward to the challenges that it presented. However not all stress comes from work and hence I looked more broadly at my life to see if there were other events which may have been prolonged enough and stressful enough to be a trigger in the development of my cancer.

Similarly, I looked at anger or unhappiness as a possible cause of my cancer. I of course have been known to have the occasional outbursts of anger, which I usually regret. These outbursts are rare and I think would be classed as fairly mild outbursts. I would generally not direct them towards people around me. My outbursts would more likely be about some injustice or some problem that is hurting people, particularly if a solution looks possible but is being ignored or rejected because it doesn't suit the priorities, aspirations or politics of someone or some group. I don't class these outbursts of anger as constituting the type of anger which researchers say impacts adversely on health. Similarly I am not an unhappy person. I greet each day with enthusiasm (even when it means getting up from a warm bed and going outside in the frost for my morning run). I have always been optimistic and positive. I enjoy humour and laughter and delight in telling jokes. Grumpy is not my style.

However, while I was at first inclined to dismiss unhappiness as a cause, I did acknowledge that there was a period in my life when I was extremely unhappy. What I needed to explore was whether this period was significant enough to contribute to cancer development.

This period was marked by increasing unhappiness, frustration and stress. This was a time when a marriage of over 30 years began to progressively unwind, and I felt powerless to do anything to stop the disintegration. I was aware at the time of the emotions and feelings generated by the increasingly difficult relationship, but I didn't realise until much later of how deeply I had been affected, physically and mentally.

The difficulties in the relationship developed slowly, and at first it was possible to ignore or dismiss them. I had tried unsuccessfully many times to make changes in the relationship, but there came a time in the breakdown when the situation was extremely difficult and I became very adept at avoiding the conflict. One of the strategies I used was to stay at work for longer and longer. I chose weekend work and late evening finishing times rather than be at home – after all, I enjoyed my work and home meant conflict. Each evening when I drove home, about half a kilometre from my house, I would suddenly feel extremely tense and stressed. I used distraction at times as a strategy but I found avoidance the best way to handle the increasing difficulties associated with the decline in the relationship. I knew from experience that calm or sensible discussion was impossible, as it would always result in confrontation, disagreement and increased tension, and so avoidance was the best strategy, even though some degree of tension and stress was always present.

During this period of extreme tension I had my annual visit to my doctor for a check-up. This had always been preceded by a blood test and had in the past been a positive and affirmative experience because I always had very good results and was buoyed by being deemed so healthy. However, on this occasion my doctor was alarmed and wanted to know what was happening in my life. These were not the test results of a healthy person. I was advised to make some changes quickly to my life or my health could suffer, and that if I didn't, I could suffer a heart attack or have a stroke.

I now know from my reading that the considerable body of evidence from scientific experiments demonstrates that fear, frustration and stress produce toxins that can cause significant damage to health. Although my relationship was very stressful, I felt that by immersing myself in my work I was making significant achievements, which further reinforced my need to work long hours. However, what the doctor had said to me made me think again. Clearly the situation was damaging to my physical and mental health. I was forced to confront the reality that I was not immune from the damage caused by prolonged exposure to fear, anxiety and stress (in this context by fear I mean the fear of losing something that is important and that I had invested a lot in). Such exposure is not compatible with good health – my good health.

My immediate thoughts were to see if I could devise better avoidance strategies. The alternative was to remove myself from the toxic environment, but this seemed too difficult to contemplate. However I kept getting messages – in different ways – that were telling me to take steps to protect my health. For example soon after I visited the doctor I was reading some journal articles which unexpectedly made reference to the negative consequences for health when fear, anxiety and stress are combined with feelings of lack of love, support and understanding. It was not very long after being confronted with a dramatic decline in my health indicators that separation occurred. This was one of the most difficult decisions in my life. The act of separation was stressful, but seemed to be less stressful than continuing to try to find new avoidance strategies and risk doing further damage to my health

I was very surprised to find that I immediately felt an enormous sense of relief. I was also able to see clearly for the first time just how stressful the situation had been – much more stressful than I had realised when I was immersed in the relationship. I was also able to see just how incredibly dysfunctional the relationship had become. Although I felt regret and some sadness, this was not overwhelming and I believe that I had already been grieving the loss of that relationship for quite some time as it was declining and disintegrating.

I was now in a new place physically and mentally and couldn't believe how wonderful I felt. My next visit to my doctor was very different to the previous one. I was back to being a good example of a healthy person. I moved on with life very effortlessly and found work to be easier, old friendships continued and new ones emerged and my running improved. In fact I found a new and fresh commitment to running and I was able to successfully complete some serious mountain-running challenges soon after the separation. Running also brought me a new sense of joy and freedom.

You may recall that I commented earlier that when my cancer was diagnosed I was advised that it had been there for a number of years, growing slowly, and by the time it was discovered was rather large. It is thus possible that the stress from a dysfunctional relationship had been the trigger for the start of creating the right conditions for my cancer to form and then slowly grow.

I also mentioned earlier about being advised that the process leading to cancer usually involves the development of a precancerous growth (polyp), which may become cancerous. I indicated in Chapter 4 that rectal cancer grows slowly in stages, firstly in the lining of the rectum and then as it develops it grows into the deeper layers of the rectum. It seems to me that the very stressful period in my life occurred at about the right time for it to be the trigger for the growth of a polyp and then eventually the start of a cancer.

Although including details about my marriage breakdown was a painful and difficult decision, I have included it to illustrate the point that events and situations can trigger health problems. In my case the relationship became toxic and that situation persisted for a long time. It's hard for me to identify an exact point in the relationship when it started to become stressful. In retrospect I can see that there had been a gradual deterioration in the relationship, leading eventually to patterns of behaviour that created anxiety and stress.

This is not about blame, or right or wrong, but about what a prolonged stressful situation can do to health. In fact, I could probably say that in one sense I caused the breakdown because I changed how I operated within the relationship. I had for a long time hoped for a closer, more intimate, relationship involving a greater level of affection, openness and companionship, and believed that in time that would eventuate.

My behaviour within the relationship had neurotic elements. I believed that I had the capacity to be the best husband possible and that if anyone could make the relationship work it was me. All I had to do was work harder and put a little more effort in to demonstrate what a wonderful husband I was. So, for a long time, that is what I did. But nothing changed.

I had a very nice house, no financial problems, four wonderful children and a great job, but I was unhappy. Unhappy because I couldn't understand why there was no change in the relationship. After the children left home, and the involvement in their education and activities (sport, cubs/scouts, music etc.) ceased, the relationship was even more exposed to examination.

My pride told me I should have been able to make it work but I had failed. I started to look for other explanations and to examine the question of happiness. A whole new phase in my understanding and personal growth started.

My first encounter was with one of the books by Andrew Matthews: *Being Happy.* This had an immediate impact on my understanding about my behaviour and started a personal journey, which, I am pleased to report, still continues thanks to the help of many brilliant writers and through sharing with others who have been on similar journeys. The consequence of starting my personal journey is that I soon made changes, including ceasing my neurotic behaviour. That's when the relationship started to unravel.

I continued to read and explore; to find new personal challenges and insights. But I stopped sharing these exciting revelations as they only caused conflict. It's interesting that when I separated I was partway through reading a wonderful book by David Schnarch: *Passionate Marriage*. Schnarch emphasised the need for individuals to be 'differentiated' within relationships, particularly if a relationship is of tremendous emotional significance. He spends the remainder of the book explaining and applying this within a relationship. Many works that I have consulted frequently comment that going forward with personal growth often comes at a cost. The cost may be in having to abandon cherished beliefs or the self you have created to become the person you truly are, or leave relationships that are flawed and are not fixable.

Hence the consequence of the disintegration of the relationship involved, for me, increasing stress at a significant level. As I indicated above, I believe that, for me, it was possible that living for a prolonged period in an environment that was very stressful led to the release of toxins that were potentially powerful enough to cause a major health problem. It's also possible that by the time I had moved away from the stress of the relationship the damage was already done and the cancer was slowly starting to grow. This of course is speculation, but it is based on lots of research about the possible impact of stress, anxiety and fear, and my deep feelings about what was happening to me during that period of my life.

In exploring the cause of my cancer I have been curious about what part the immune system plays in disease prevention. I am aware that it is a complex and wonderful system. In my discussion I have focussed on the impact of events that caused stress, anger and unhappiness, which, in turn, may cause health problems. Some writers talk about the impact of these types of events on the mind and how this can cause cancer and other diseases. In my case this would mean that the events I described above could have had a negative impact over a significant period on my mind, which then influenced my body's defence mechanisms. This approach is summarised by (Dr) Deepak Chopra as follows:

> *In mind-body medicine, any explanation has its roots in an earlier stage, in a moment when the immune system was weakened by a negative mental influence.*

The body's defence mechanisms are clearly very important in protecting us from illness and disease. The factors that I mentioned above that may cause disease (including cancer) may not succeed because of the operation of our defence mechanisms. These mechanisms are clearly very important in keeping us healthy. Thus it seems that it's possible for the mind to negatively influence the operation of the defence mechanism. This impact can apparently be profound in terms of our wellbeing. This is expressed by Chopra as follows:

> *How infinitely beautiful the immune system is and how terribly vulnerable at the same time. It forges our link with life and yet can break it at any moment. The immune system knows all our secrets, all our sorrows. It knows why a mother who has lost a child can die of grief, because the immune system has died of grief first. It knows every moment a cancer patient spends in the light of life or the shadow of death, because it turns these moments into the body's physical reality.*

Clearly I won't ever know with certainty why I developed rectal cancer. As discussed in this chapter, there are many factors that can have a negative impact on health. Some of these deal with physical health and others deal with the mind. In my case I believe that I had taken good care of my physical needs through a healthy lifestyle, but

I fear that I had not paid sufficient attention to the importance of mind matters. While I was aware of the importance of the mind in regard to health I clearly underestimated the significance it played in my health. It seems that good health involves much more than good food, regular exercise and the absence of harmful substances. I have come to the conclusion that if we neglect the role of our minds in maintaining good health and wellbeing we possibly do so at our peril. Hence it seems that attending to a combination of physical and mental (mind) matters is vital if we are to avoid major health problems.

Chapter 8

Why did I Survive?

*I am that supreme and fiery force that sends forth all
the sparks of life. Death hath no part of me, yet do I
allot it, wherefore I am girt about with wisdom as
with wings. I am that living and fiery essence of the
divine substance that flows in the beauty of the fields.
I shine in water, I burn in the sun and the moon and
the stars. Mine is the mysterious force of the invisible
wind … I am life.*

Hildegarde of Bingen (1098–1179)

Given that my rectal cancer was large, had been present for a long
time and had escaped into my lymph nodes, survival was not
guaranteed. The survival rate from colorectal cancer is improving
largely because of earlier detection. Survival apparently depends on a
number of factors, including age, state of health, stage of the disease
when diagnosed, and if it has recurred. Of these factors the stage
of the disease on diagnosis seems to be very important to survival.
Figures published by several sources show the following survival
rates (based on survival for five years after diagnosis):

- 90% where the cancer was localised (contained within the tissue of the rectum or colon)
- 68% where the cancer is regional (had spread to the lymph nodes)
- 10% where the cancer was distant (had metastasised i.e. spread to another non-adjacent organ or organs).

There is a higher success rate if the cancer is detected early (it seems that only about 40 per cent are in fact detected early). In some two-thirds of colorectal cancer cases the cancer is located in the colon and for the remaining third its located in the rectum.

Colorectal cancer is Australia's second most common cancer and is common in both men and women. It comprises about 13 per cent of all cancers diagnosed (9 per cent is the international figure). It seems to be largely a disease of developed countries with high rates in Australia, United States, Canada, New Zealand and Western Europe. Each year a number of people die from colorectal cancer. Given that my cancer was large and had escaped the rectum into the lymph nodes I have wondered why I survived. In addition to the cancer I had significant complications, including septicaemia, pneumonia and major temperature and liver problems. Septicaemia alone can cause death and almost did in my case (so I am told).

Clearly there could be lots of reasons for survival and it could be said that there is no simple answer to this question. However I believe that in my case that, despite my condition and the complications, I chose life. This may sound like a strange thing to say. Clearly then if survival is that simple why wouldn't all people with a potentially terminal illness put up their hands and elect to live? Having made that statement let me try to explain.

Firstly I do need to acknowledge that I did have excellent medical care. All of my doctors were skilled and dedicated. The nursing staff were likewise extremely good at their work and very caring and supportive. I also had support from a range of allied health workers (e.g. physiotherapist, dietitian). The hospital facilities were also very good. I am sure that without the continuing care and intervention of all these people and access to the facilities I would have died. However, many people receive the same level of care as me and yet die. Some might conclude that this is fate or bad luck.

As I commented in the previous chapter, I believe that we can create illness in our bodies – or at least we can create the conditions for an illness to develop. In that chapter I also explored the circumstances relating to my cancer and concluded that the conditions for its development likely arose during a period of sustained stress, and that my high level of fitness wasn't sufficient to prevent the development of cancer (I will return to this point in the context of some comments on prevention). Thus if we can create the circumstances to cause an illness in our bodies then it may be possible to create conditions to cure that illness, or at least to aid the cure or even to complement the treatment in a way that ensures or maximises the chance of a successful outcome.

At no stage during my illness did I believe that I would not recover. When I was diagnosed I was in temporary shock and disbelief and possibly my pride was damaged. As I have commented several times, how could anyone as fit and healthy as me, and who repeatedly scored well in health assessments, possibly have cancer? However, I was quickly forced to leave these thoughts behind and move to a position of feeling that this may be unpleasant, it may be difficult, it may be painful but I will be fine. In fact, as time went by and the treatment became more invasive, complex, unpleasant and difficult, I was even stronger in my belief and resolve and was confident that I would recover.

Penny tells a story of an incident that took place in the ICU, which she believes illustrates my belief that I would be fine. It was a couple of days after I had been awoken from my four-day period of induced sleep following life-saving surgery, and I lay connected to an array of apparatus, with multiple tubes coming from various parts of my body. A team of concerned specialists had just finished a consultation about me at the end of my bed. In a conversation with

Penny she commented that I was very ill but had passed a critical point. I reacted immediately by forcefully telling her that I was not ill. I did not see myself as a sick person. In my mind I was in a phase of my treatment that was required at that point and that I would soon move onto the next phase in my treatment and full recovery.

This incident has become a little bit of a joke amongst my friends, some of whom were outside the ICU and heard about it from Penny soon after it occurred. Clearly the doctors at that time were concerned about the state of my health, as were my family and friends. However, although I felt pain and discomfort and was unable to undertake even the simplest function without help, I didn't consider myself to be ill. The other people in the ICU may have been ill but I wasn't. I saw what was happening to me as necessary; that this was a temporary situation that would pass and I would be fine. I had lots of time (day and night) to dwell on my state of health. In fact it was difficult at times, particularly in the middle of the night, not to think about it. It's also easy to get drawn into negative thinking when progress is slow and there are frequent setbacks. However, my thinking was never within a sickness paradigm but rather within a healing/wellness paradigm.

I have found it interesting to investigate how positive thinking as an aid to recovery is viewed by the medical profession. I discovered that a considerable amount has been written on the subject, including a number of studies designed to investigate the matter. It seems that some of the early studies were designed to demonstrate that a patient's mental state had no bearing on the outcome. An early study conducted by Stanford University was one such study. In fact, it found the opposite. Those patients in the group that received a small amount of counselling support to improve their thinking about their situation lived twice as long as those in the group that received no support. There have been many other studies that have supported this conclusion. Despite this I understand that there are some people within the medical profession that are sceptical about the contribution that positive thinking can make to healing and survival.

I believe that it made a significant difference to me, not only in my recovery but also to the speed of my recovery. One person who has written extensively on the importance of our emotional state on health, recovery and life, is medical practitioner Deepak Chopra who concludes that: *'Emotions are the fundamental stuff of life'*.

I have been an avid reader of Deepak Chopra's writings for many years and have found his work to be thought provoking, useful, challenging and practical.

Related to this question of emotional state and its importance to recovering from illness is the question of how we view ourselves, particularly the value we place on our self. Do I love myself? Do I approve of myself and do I have a high level of self-acceptance? I previously discussed this in the context of causing an illness, but what about its importance in the healing process. I believe that we are each responsible for our own happiness, wellbeing and health. I further believe that placing a high level of value on myself is an important component in my ability to fulfilling this responsibility. Unfortunately we are often taught as children that loving ourselves is somehow an undesirable thing and that people who love themselves are egotistical. As adults we often don't change our thinking or understanding of this important matter. The result is a very superficial and simplistic understanding of what loving our self really means. This can also be mixed up and further confused with feeling of inadequacy and even self-hatred.

To repeat what I said previously, when I think about loving myself I am not thinking about vanity or arrogance, as these are not love but rather negative feelings that are derived from fear and anger. When I talk about self-love I am referring to my uniqueness as an individual and about celebrating the miracle that created me, including my body and mind. Through this perspective I see myself as being worthy and of great value. Our subconscious mind can so easily be trained by us to believe that we are inadequate.

However I know from my experience that a feeling of inadequacy is only a thought and thoughts can be changed (if that's what we desire). It of course helps if others affirm me as a valuable person. The valuing process often starts with our parents. I was fortunate to have wonderful parents who told me and demonstrated through their actions that I was of great value. My concept of self-love has of course changed over the years as I have grown to understand myself more deeply and my role in achieving good health. I believe that the value I placed upon myself was an important factor in the process of my recovery and healing, despite difficult times during the process. Had I thought about myself as worthless or inadequate I am sure that those negative feelings would have been detrimental to my recovery.

The feelings I had about myself were reinforced many times by the words and actions of family and friends. I am very fortunate to have a wonderfully supportive wife and family and a large number of extraordinary friends. Penny spent many hours at my bedside during each of my periods in hospital, including sleeping at the hospital in order to provide, through love, a huge amount of support when I was clearly unwell and unable to undertake the simplest of self-care functions. It was enormously reassuring to have her there. She was there not at my request but because she wanted to be with me, share my difficulties and provide support. Although at one very low point she was advised that there was a strong possibility that I would not survive surgery she remained optimistic. She knew that I believed that I would be fine and she reinforced my belief with her actions.

The support provided by our friends, including the love and care shown to Penny, was enormously helpful in my healing process. It also enabled her to continue to support me, day after day. While I have previously mentioned the importance of friendships I feel I need to underline their significance in the healing process. The friendships existed before the cancer but this was a time when many friendships deepened considerably. I know that this was the case because I witnessed feelings being expressed openly, without embarrassment and with great joy. In the context of my healing this brought a sense of liberation as I saw how the open expressions of love were able to occur, particularly with my male friends. I can't recall a time prior to my illness when I was hugged, touched and kissed so much by so many of my friends, including my male friends. It was a wonderful reinforcement of my worth and a very good reason to survive.

Throughout the duration of my health problems I received many cards, letters, messages, gifts and flowers from a wide range of people, including many who lived in other places. Their messages were supportive, caring, encouraging and positive. I had many people tell me how they had valued working with me and about the contributions I had made in some aspect of work. Each time I entered hospital a new batch of communications would arrive. I mentioned in a previous chapter how I recall vividly an occasion when I was sitting (rather uncomfortably and reluctantly) in a chair in the ICU and Penny presented me with an enormous bundle of unopened mail. Reading the messages led me to burst into tears. The tears streamed down my face and I was unable to stop crying. I was deeply overcome by the feeling that so many people were concerned about my welfare. Some told me that they were sending positive thoughts to me; others said they had prayed for me; and some had crafted some special words, which were wonderful to receive. With so many people and so many different approaches I think just about every possible base was covered.

I have read about people being stigmatised and abandoned following a cancer diagnosis. One such story was about the experience of woman who told about being abandoned and feeling like she had left the community of the well and entered the desert of the diseased. Just when she needed emotional support she felt alone because her friends began to withdraw and act inappropriately when they learnt of her cancer diagnosis.

Penny and I often commented that experiencing what we had both experienced (the initial shock, the various treatments, the many ups and downs) would have been extremely difficulty without the support of family and friends. I have also often thought how difficult I would have found it without Penny. To be alone and to experience what I experienced would have been very challenging.

I decided during each of my periods in hospital that it would be important for my recovery – as well as being polite – to respond to every card, letter, message and phone call. It was usually a few weeks after discharge from hospital each time that I had the strength and concentration to respond to each message. In each case I wrote a thank you note and commented upon my progress. This became an important activity for me and I wanted the readers to know how important their thoughts, messages, prayers and good wishes had been to me. In some cases I was able to comment that when the message arrived I was about to undergo or had just undergone some procedure and that what they had said stayed with me during the procedure or the recovery. At times my letters of thanks led to further communications. Although I could usually only do one or two of these a day because I was too tired and felt too unwell, I nevertheless felt that this was important and was contributing to my mental and physical healing.

In the spiritual domain there are many practices that help people survive and cope with a major health problem. These involve connection with some higher source through a process such as prayer or meditation. I was clearly prayed for many times during my health problems, particularly each time I was hospitalised. I don't know exactly what was contained in those prayers but I am sure that they were a genuine call for intervention on my behalf. I suspect that some would have asked for me to be cured of my cancer, others possibly asked that the doctors, nurses and health workers treating me be supported to exercise the highest level of skill and care in administering the treatment, while some may have asked that I be given the strength to cope with the treatment I was receiving. For me knowing that a range of different people with different beliefs systems were praying for me was affirming and no doubt was important to my positive thinking and in my healing.

Clearly there would be those who would reject this as unhelpful and not consistent with their belief system and I respect that viewpoint. However I was open to accepting the intervention others were making on my behalf without necessarily needing to share their beliefs. I don't wish to comment any further on different belief systems here as I don't think this is the place for such a discussion, but the point I want to make is that I believe openness is very important to healing. Without openness we can create blockages and rigidity that is not helpful in the healing process. In ancient China the Tao Te Ching proclaimed:

> *Whatever is flexible and flowering will tend to grow,*
> *whatever is rigid and blocked will wither and die.*

I do believe that we all have many dimensions and one of these is what we might describe as a spiritual dimension. My spiritual journey, like many other aspects of my personal journey, is very much a work in progress. Many of my values and beliefs came from my parents. I observed them assisting many family members, friends and neighbours and contributing in many ways to the local community. They both gave generously in their work for the community and received recognition, although that recognition was not the motivation. They lived in a small town and were part of a church community and many clubs and groups. Growing up in this environment made it impossible for me not to absorb some of their values and their very positive no-nonsense approach to life.

As part of my personal growth I have questioned many of my beliefs and certainly have questioned things I learnt as a child. I think questioning is an essential part of growth. As part of my journey I have looked at the work of modern theologians as part of this process of attempting to understand and find relevance for me, just as I have read the works of many teachers and also the thoughts and values of individuals who have had an impact for good. I believe that I have a responsibility to continue to search for the answers to significant questions and that this is very important to my happiness and health. Many faiths, religions and teachers have made similar statements. For example the Dalia Lama said:

> *I believe that the very purpose of our life is to seek happiness.*

During my illness I had lots of time to think and reflect and I found my thoughts often returned to my belief that I needed to take responsibility for my health and happiness. It can be challenging to think about health and happiness when you are unwell and in the middle of a major health problem. However I found it very helpful particularly at those times when another setback in recovery had occurred. I didn't pray for myself – I left that to others – but I did remind myself that it was my responsibility to get well, to get out of hospital and to rehabilitate myself. I had a belief that I had a significant part to play in my recovery.

At the beginning of this chapter I spoke about choosing life being a reason why I survived cancer and the many complications that arose along the way. I have no doubt that a positive attitude and a strong desire to survive were significant in my survival, recovery and rehabilitation, although I can't help feeling that my survival was somewhat more complex than that. I have a strong sense that knowing that I was deeply loved had an enormous impact on my survival. My experience seems to support the findings of many studies into survival that have found that love and intimacy play a powerful part in health, wellbeing and survival. There are, for example, lots of epidemiology studies into the patterns, causes, and effects of health and disease conditions in defined populations that provide clear evidence that love, intimacy and social support lead to health, joy and healing. However, the exact reason why these factors are so important appears to be something of a mystery. Clearly I had lots of support, love and care, which I was always extremely conscious of. At another level and returning to my role in this it seems possible that intimacy is also about my relationship with myself – having a sense of self and understanding who I am.

Who I am involves understanding the relationship between body, mind, soul and spirit and the fact that they are not separate but all related and part of a whole, which is me. When I have thought about this in an open way and experienced a sense of wholeness I have felt more able to readily meet health challenges in a new way that seems to incorporate a sense of renewal, nurturing and restoration. I think this is what I meant by reference to my survival and recovery being somewhat more complex than simply my optimism. It would seem that I have a lot more exploring to do to try and understand this a little better, particularly to understand the implications for future health, happiness and my ongoing journey in discovering the person I truly am (the real me). For this to happen I will need to be open to all possibilities.

I will leave the last words in this chapter to a 13th century Sufi poet, Rumi, when he wrote:

> *There is a community of the spirit.*
> *Join it, and feel the delight of walking*
> *in the noisy street,*
> *And being the noise …*
> *Why do you stay in prison*
> *when the door is wide open?*
> *Move outside the tangle of fear-thinking.*
> *Live in silence.*
> *Flow down and down in always*
> *Widening rings of being.*

Chapter 9

What Have I Learnt?

It's a funny thing, life. If you refuse to accept anything but the best you very often get it.

W Somerset Maugham

Clearly it would be a pity to get cancer, have a number of surgical interventions, six months of chemotherapy, a program of radiotherapy, many setbacks (including almost dying) and not gain something from it (other than many scars and lots of images of painful experiences). A little bit of wisdom or some personal insights or growth would be nice. As TS Elliot said: *'we had the experience but missed the meaning'.*

What did this mean for me? What did I learn? Was this a life-changing experience?

The more I think about these questions and reflect on what occurred, and what has happened since the conclusion of my treatment, the more things I find I have learnt. Possibly I had lots to learn. Some of these learnings are about gaining insights from new experiences; while others are a little more significant in that some windows or doors were opened that have offered new understandings into myself. Once those doors and windows were opened I found it impossible to shut them again.

At one practical level I have learnt a lot about health matters and processes. For example, what it's like to have a major health problem and about treatment processes involved. I have learnt lots about my ability to cope with discomfort and pain. I had never been a patient in a hospital before my first surgery to remove the cancer. I now know lots about being in hospital. On the lighter side I was very particular about my privacy before this all started. Within a very short period of time I was very relaxed about being showered, examined and exposed. I recall walking around the hospital pushing my saline drip and dragging several drainage bags during my daily 'exercise' and having Penny tell me to do up the back of my hospital gown. I was apparently exposing my backside, which I was unconcerned about (you might conclude too much morphine was involved). Possibly strange behaviour for someone who only a short time previously had been very particular about his privacy. I think I was learning another lesson about what is really important in life (I am sure that I have a few more of these lessons to learn).

At a more profound level I have learnt that life is very valuable. However it's not something that is so valuable that it needs to be wrapped in cotton wool or locked away. On the contrary it needs to be lived and this can only happen by doing it. I have learnt to view each day as another opportunity to live life. I find that it's good to remind myself of this first thing each morning. It's become a little bit like a mantra to me. It's easy to forget and so a daily reminder is valuable. No matter what the weather is like or what lies ahead for the day I believe it's a great way to start the day. Clearly if I am going to get on with my life then I need to be proactive. I can't live life by sitting at home wondering if someone will call. Even if it's not physically possible to get out it is possible to call a friend or do something meaningful. I am fortunate because for me living life can involve an enormous array of possibilities.

I also decided that whatever I do needs to be done in a joyful way. I now find that the things that I need to do in life are enhanced if I look forward to them. This has involved me re-examining how I view the mundane things in life, such as paying the bills, cleaning, gardening and shopping for the groceries. I needed to do this because for most of us all of these activities are part of real life and are therefore important and need to be seen in that context. I find that if I view them as important (even if not exciting) then they seem easier to achieve and will contribute to the day rather than becoming a chore. I decided that I needed to be creative about how I think about my life and, as a result, more meanings and opportunities seem to emerge.

As I have said, almost immediately after being diagnosed I was confronted with the fact that I had cancer even though I was extremely fit and had not been ill for years. I was used to people telling me what a fantastic example of a healthy, fit person I was, and how fit and healthy I looked for my age (always good to hear), and this had fed my ego from which I derived a sense of superiority.

Eckhart Tolle, in his book *A New Earth*, discusses at length the ego and at one point talks about the importance of identification for our ego. Clearly my identification as a super-fit, super-healthy person was great reinforcement for my ego. I had a terrible thought after my diagnosis about how would I be able to admit to all these people that I had cancer. Hence one of my early learnings was the realisation that I needed to deal with this. If I didn't deal with it then it would become a barrier to my recovery, personal growth and friendships. I firstly had to admit that letting go of this image would not diminish who I am. This involved accepting this loss of image, which took me beyond my ego to who I really am. Doing this was liberating and a great lesson for me in how to let go of things and be more open to new possibilities. I still need to work on this because my ego is always looking for an opportunity to reassert itself and gain a predominant place in my thoughts. As soon as I am conscious of this I smile to myself and my ego is put back in its box. I am of course still very interested in being healthy but I no longer identify with this illusion of who I am.

I indicated in a previous chapter that positive thinking was important in enabling me to cope with the many ups and downs of my illness, the many interventions and treatments that were required, and in the survival and healing processes. It was sometimes a challenge to be positive in the face of some unpleasant and painful experiences. At these times I often needed to do some self-talk as a way of maintaining a positive outlook. Although I am an optimistic person I have learnt that being positive in the face of adversity can sometimes be a challenge.

For me the key was often about controlling my thought processes. I couldn't control others or the environment but I did have the potential to control my thoughts. How I thought about circumstances and events determined the impact they had on me and the feelings that resulted from my thinking. If I didn't exercise control of my thinking then my mind would go to the default position, which was about looking for an easy way out (the 'I wish' type of thinking). This type of thinking leads to hoping for a change of circumstances (I wish that I was no longer ill or that I could avoid some intervention). This type of thinking is clearly unhelpful, particularly as it doesn't lead to a change and doesn't have a calming effect. I needed to be able to focus my thoughts on equipping me to be able to deal with the situation. This involved having a new mindset, which was about being positive and believing that I could have some control over my situation by how I thought about it. I always believed that I would be cured of cancer and would survive the many setbacks that arose along the way.

If your thought processes are like mine then unfortunately they are probably often coloured by past experiences, which can lock our minds into predictable patterns of behaviour. Some of these patterns are in the subconscious and were developed when we were children. This means that we are often unaware of them even though they determine how we will respond to a situation.

This can dictate our attitudes, assumptions, beliefs and reactions. When these are negative then we may have a negative response, which is often destructive. However when our mental patterns are constructive we can be motivated towards self-enhancing thinking and behaviour. I often had to remind myself that these are only thoughts and they can be changed which means that each time I did this I was in effect reprogramming my subconscious mind to think positively and believe that anything is possible. While this will require an understanding of self and may require some practice and reinforcement I have found this process to be enormously helpful in reinforcing positive thinking each day. If I have negative thoughts I try to immediately be aware that this is happening, to then name it as destructive and replace it with the opposite type of thought. This works for me but it does take ongoing practice or the mind will easily revert to old ways.

On a related matter I was confronted many times with situations that required unpleasant procedures that often involved dealing with pain. I can't claim that I looked forward to pain but I do understand that it's inevitable in circumstances where you have a major health problem. It's also an indicator that you are alive! However I believe that this didn't mean that I needed to put up with pain or that there were not ways of dealing with it or at least ameliorating it. Clearly I had access to medication to deal with or ease pain. I woke up each time after surgery with a device that would administer morphine if I decided to press a button. I did not like using the morphine and always asked for it to be taken away fairly soon after the surgery. Morphine certainly took away pain but it made me feel very tired, affected my mental processes and had some kind of negative impact on my personality (such as becoming less positive and having black thoughts). I was more interested in exploring other ways of dealing with pain. I understand that without the nerve signals that transmit pain there is no pain.

The mind-body medicine revolution that I mentioned previously was based on the simple discovery that the mind can be used to create healing and wellness as well as to create disease. Hence the mind can be used to create endorphins (which long distance runners are familiar with) that will fit into pain receptors to block pain. I had previously explored the mind-body relationship through the work of a number of people writing about personal growth, health, healing, peace and happiness. There have been lots of experiments in this area, including giving people a placebo in the place of pain-relief drugs, with the result that large numbers experienced the same pain relief as if they had taken a pain-killing drug.

I had in the past experimented with using my mind to stop pain. For example I no longer get headaches because I practiced using my subconscious mind to program out headaches. If I get the slightest inkling that a headache may be coming on then I quickly do some mind work to stop it from developing. This always works for me but it did take some practice and I had some failures initially. Being familiar with this I attempted to use it when I was confronted with a potentially painful experience in hospital. At times this was relatively effective and at other times I found it to be more difficult, particularly when I was really unwell and struggling to focus. At these times I had to stop myself from wishing that I could change my circumstances (be someplace else, not be ill) and I had to remind myself to focus so that I could handle the pain. I found this to be very helpful.

I also tried to visualise any painful experience as taking me a step closer to complete healing. I had also to remind myself that it was very important to be in the now. I tried to recall what Eckhart Tolle had written about the impact of this and how dysfunction and pain can set in when we are not in the now. Tolle sees this as being transformative:

> *Whatever the present moment contains, accept it as if you had chosen it. Work with it not against it. Make it your friend and ally, not your enemy. This will miraculously transform your whole life.*

Hence I believe that I learnt some different ways of handling pain, which were about making significant changes to how I operated. For this to work then some reprogramming of the subconscious is required, together with lots of practice and lots of reinforcement. In retrospect I have at times thought that this process is much like training for a marathon. The training involves training the mind as well as training the body to withstand the physical demands of an endurance event like a marathon. The long training runs in preparation for a marathon are as much mental as physical. No matter how well you prepare it will always hurt during the last 10 kilometres or so. It doesn't matter if you are a novice marathoner or an elite runner you will always experience pain in the last part of the event. It's at this point that the mind becomes extremely important in determining how or if you will finish. The mind can start giving you messages about stopping (it's okay to stop, you don't need to do this, you can do this some other time). That's when you need to be in the moment, be clear that you have trained well and be confident that you can finish. At the start of a marathon I have often looked around me and thought that there will be a number in the group who won't finish and others will finish badly, barely able to walk. Some of those won't have prepared properly, others will have been foolish and started too quickly and some will succumb to negative thinking. I think being an experienced marathoner helped me to understand the importance of being in the moment and the power of the mind, and was helpful during my times in hospital dealing with many unpleasant events and procedures.

I have said many times in this book that I believe being happy was important to my health and in my recovery from illness. I have learnt that this doesn't just happen, that it's complex and that happiness can mean different things to different people. And it can be hard to focus on happiness in the middle of a major health problem. However I am sure that it's important to wellbeing and that I made the decision (at times with some difficulty) to take responsibility for my happiness and do something about it (including exploring its meaning for me). Making changes in the way I operated started with a decision to change. Abraham Lincoln once said:

> *Most people are about as happy as they make up their mind to be.*

Hugh Mackay, a researcher, teacher and writer in social science, talks about happiness in the context of leading the good life. He sees a good life as being a valuable life, a life that contributes to the wellbeing of others. He sees this as being manifested by us when we can demonstrate our commitment to 'taking other people seriously, respecting them and acknowledging their desire for proper recognition'. Mackay's research has led him to conclude that each person wants to be 'acknowledged, respected, appreciated, understood, valued and accepted'. In order to lead the good life by contributing to the wellbeing of others we need to demonstrate our commitment by listening attentively (the gift of undivided attention), apologise sincerely when we have hurt, offended, wronged or upset someone (humility and courage required) and generously forgive (demonstrate compassion). As Mackay notes:

> *Attentive listening, sincere apology, generous forgiveness: these are the gifts we most want from others and, therefore, the gifts we should be most willing to give to others. These are indeed the three great therapies of everyday life.*

Mackay then adds that there is another component of living the good life, which he says is to 'make 'em laugh'. He sees this as being able to be a person of good humour ('a sense of humour is one of the attributes humans rate most highly'). To demonstrate this requires a smile and a willingness to see that 'life is often amusing and sometimes delightfully, unimaginably absurd'. When times are difficult, such as during an illness, laughter releases endorphins that raise the pain threshold and reduce stress. He concludes that we should all be 'grateful to anyone who can trigger that magical response in us'.

I enjoy going to the movies but tend to miss a number and so I always have a list of movies I want to see. I was reflecting recently on what Hugh Mackay had to say when I was in a position to see one of those movies on my list. The movie, *The Bucket List*, was released in 2007 and so it has taken me a long while to catch up with it. It's the story of Carter (Morgan Freeman), a motor mechanic, and Edward (Jack Nicholson), a billionaire hospital magnate. They are both diagnosed with terminal cancer and despite their vast differences in background and values their relationship develops. It's a feel-good movie and while some critics have criticised it for a number of reasons I am pleased that I got to see it. It raised for me a number of important issues that Mackay raised in his book about friendship, happiness and leading a good life. Carter tried to get his new friend Edward to think about what brings joy. At one point he says that in ancient Egypt the people believed that the Egyptian Gods would pose two questions to those entering heaven: 'Have you found joy in your life?' and 'Has your life brought joy to others?'. Joy is a concept that Edward has difficulty with. Carter persists with this by leaving a note for Edward, which said: 'I am going to ask you to do one more thing for me – find joy in your life'. Near the end Carter professes a belief in God whereas Edward admits that he has trouble with the concept. His belief is: 'we live and we die and the wheels on the bus go round and round'. At the end of the movie we are left with joy and faith, two important issues to grapple with.

Clearly we all make choices about how we decide to deal with the challenges involved in life. During my time with cancer, for me being happy involved being positive. I know through experience that being happy is not always easy, and that being happy can be a significant challenge. Staying positive in these circumstances required me to do lots of work with my thinking. This involved dealing quickly with any black thoughts so that I didn't focus on what was wrong. I was aware that I was responsible for what I thought. I could therefore choose to focus on happy and positive things if I wished. This involved some discipline in being alert so that I didn't let the negative creep in and swamp my thinking.

At times in hospital I had lots of reasons to think about the negative but I was determined to stay focussed on the positive. I found lots of positive things to focus on including simple things like the smile from one of the nurses, the things that had been said to me by friends and family, the care being provided or the tea lady simply saying 'Hello love, how are you today?'. In some cases it is just a matter of deciding that you don't want to be unhappy any more. It's remarkable how things look different once a decision to be happy has been made. For me being happy involved lots of maintenance work. In other words I needed to remind myself periodically that I had decided to be happy and to focus on the good things in my life and around me. I am sure that being happy while I was in hospital was very important in assisting me to deal with some significant health problems and face many unpleasant interventions. If I took time to look I could always find things to be happy about and ways or strategies to be positive.

Eckhart Tolle believes that we periodically seek emotional negativity – that is, we seek unhappiness and that we need a considerable amount of awareness to see this in ourselves. Clearly this is another barrier to think about and a challenge in achieving happiness, particularly as emotional negativity is more likely in times of difficulty, such as during an illness.

I have decided that I don't want to be ill ever again. I don't even want to have a cold. While I was ill my health was clearly very important to lots of people and I clearly needed to take responsibility for it. I thought that I had been doing that prior to being diagnosed with cancer. Possibly I need to do more to ensure that I never have cancer again. As mentioned in previous chapters there is plenty of evidence to indicate that what we eat and drink are very important to our health. Likewise there is now irrefutable evidence that smoking does considerable harm to our bodies and is a major cause of or at least a contributor to the formation of cancer. As a runner I am very conscious about what has been written about the importance of regular exercise and what has been documented about health problems resulting from a lack of exercise. All these and many other factors have been reported over and over in the media and have been presented to us in numerous health prevention campaigns.

There are many reasons why some people choose to ignore this information. It's clear that some people may have limited choices possibly because of low income. One factor that seems to be a barrier for some people is that making change in lifestyle is difficult and may involve some effort (even some discomfort and pain in improving physical fitness). It seems that some people believe that although it's a bit of a gamble ignoring this evidence and the warnings that appear in the media for them it's not really a big risk. I have had some people say to me if they encounter a health problem then they will take a pill.

However, clearly for me practicing good eating habits, being a non-smoker and exercising regularly were not enough to prevent my illness. There are clearly other factors that need to be part of the mix if our choice is to be healthy. In my earlier comments about the possible causes of illness I discussed other indicators and the triggers that may cause the onset of a disease or illness. I would like to return to some of these factors and share some further thoughts about what I have learnt as a result of exploration and experiences that came from my illness, and from the questioning that I have undertaken since then.

Before I move to my first point I feel it's important to repeat that I am not dismissing the importance of good medical care in treating illness. One of my learnings following several periods in hospital, including encountering several health complications, was that good medical care was very important in my recovery. I was fortunate to have excellent medical intervention and health professionals that were competent, professional and caring people. However, I do believe that there are other factors, which are important to healing, survival and rehabilitation. They were certainly important to me.

I touched on the matter of self-love in an earlier chapter. I repeat that I am not talking about arrogance or vanity here because these are not love. I refer here to having respect for ourselves and being aware and grateful for our uniqueness as individuals. In a sense it's about the miracle that is us expressed through our body and our minds. Louise L Hall says in her book, *You Can Heal Your Life*, that on the matter of what we think of ourselves: *Love is the miracle cure.*

The flip side to this is that we don't love ourselves and this is expressed in many negative ways. For example we mistreat our bodies with food, alcohol and drugs; make poor choices that harm us; live in chaos and disorder; and attract people who are negative, unsupportive and may even abuse us. For some people making a change and loving oneself could be too risky. It may be that the bottom line is that there is a deep belief that: 'I am not good enough'. This lack of self-worth can be a major barrier to good health. If we have conditioned ourselves to believe we are unworthy, possibly because we were told that as a child, then changing this thinking may be difficult. I believe that making that change is extremely important to future health and wellbeing.

It's not my intention to discuss what I have found about changing this state of mind (there is lots written about that) but I am firmly of the view that taking a holistic view of health prevention must include dealing with the matter of self-love.

A final comment on this is that I have learnt that change is possible no matter how difficult it might seem, and that I was the only one that could make that decision to change (others couldn't decide for me and it wasn't about others changing their opinion of my worth). In terms of my illness I started with a strong sense of self-worth and continuing to believe this was important to how I acted in support of the medical processes that were undertaken to heal me. I did have negative thoughts periodically but most times I was able to deal with these quickly with some self-talk. This reinforced my positive attitude and feeling that I would be fine.

I now want to turn to love and survival. This also raises for me the other side of that equation, which is loneliness and isolation. I did touch on this in a previous discussion about the links that researchers have found between living alone and having few friends and support networks and the increased likelihood of disease and illness. It seems that loneliness is not only a factor in looking at the cause of illness and premature death but also a factor in recovery. I was very fortunate in being loved deeply and unconditionally which I believe was very important to my survival and recovery.

I have read and reread the verse contained in Sandra Boynton's book, *Consider Love*, and it always leaves me with a feeling of joy and with a large smile on my face. She starts the book with the following:

> *Consider love.*
> *Look here and there.*
> *Consider love.*
> *It's everywhere.*
> *Consider love.*
> *Observe a while.*
> *It comes in every shape, and style.*

For me love certainly came in every shape and style and it still does.

At this point in you should be in no doubt about my feelings about the importance of family and friends to me during my time with cancer and the wonderful experience I had involving the deepening of friendships. I also indicated several times that my healing process was helped enormously by the support that was provided to Penny and me. It's been well documented that relationships and networks are very important to health. I have learnt that they are also very important to healing. I vowed during one of my periods in hospital that I would cherish my friends and pay more attention to fostering and acknowledging friendships. This has become a priority for me. It seems that it's not unusual for relationships to improve and become a priority after a major event such as a health problem.

Many people have written extensively about the negative impact of loneliness and isolation on health. I briefly discussed these matters in the context of how disease and illness occurs and also in relation to surviving. While there are clearly overlaps in regard to these matters in the areas of cause and survival I want to return to loneliness and isolation in the context of insights and learning. Most writers on this subject agree that there are several ways which loneliness and isolation impact negatively on health, including by:

- increasing the likelihood of engagement in behaviours like smoking and overeating, which may directly affect health and decrease the likelihood of making lifestyle choices that are life-enhancing rather than self-destructive
- increasing the likelihood of disease and premature death from all causes by an enormous amount (some authors say by as much as 500 per cent through different mechanisms many of which are apparently not fully understood)
- fostering risky behaviour when problems arise, such as not medicating properly when an illness occurs
- preventing the experience of the joy of everyday life.

In short it seems that anything that promotes a sense of isolation often leads to illness and suffering. While on the other hand Dr Dean Ornish says that:

> *Anything that promotes a sense of love and intimacy, connection and community is healing.*

Furthermore, having a sense of meaning in the midst of an adverse event (such as a major illness) enhances survival enormously. Eckhart Tolle, in his book *The Power of Now*, talks about achieving this through being in the now, including taking control of the mind and at a deeper level learning to feel and experience the inner body.

> *Another benefit of this practice in the physical realm is a great strengthening of the immune system, which occurs when you inhabit the body. The more consciousness you bring into the body, the stronger the immune system becomes. ... It is also a potent form of self healing.*

Readers should be clear by now that I have no doubt that love and intimacy were important to my healing and survival. In thinking about this many times I have wondered if the number of relationships is important or if the quality of those relationships is more important to healing and health. I had initially come to the conclusion that in my case it was the quality of the love and intimacy that had been important to my survival. However I wasn't entirely sure what this meant and clearly I had also been supported by many people in a wide variety of ways. This led to some more thinking and exploration to see what the experience of others was.

I was able to find lots of studies (see reading list), which included an examination of the importance of relationships. They all appear to agree that relationships are important to health. For example in one study on recovery from cardiac problems it was found that men who had anxiety and family problems, especially conflict with their partners and children, had a much higher incidence of chest pain. They also looked at other risk factors and their impact on the patient and found that they were significantly moderated by a loving relationship. The studies found that having a number of relationships was helpful (assuming they are not negative relationships) but the most important factor was the depth of those relationships – how loving and supportive they were. It seems that this support must involve verbal and nonverbal communications of caring and concern, which indicates that you are valued, loved and have an opportunity for intimacy. This in turn promotes a sense of purpose, meaning and belonging, all of which are very important to healing. Put simply the researchers said that anything that promotes feelings of love and intimacy is healing and anything that promotes the opposite feelings is not.

An interesting further finding was that our immune and other defence systems are enhanced by love and relationships.

During my illness, particularly at times in hospital when complications arose, I experienced a considerable amount of love and I am sure that it was very important to my healing. While I have already commented on the importance of this to me in terms of feeling supported and aiding me to get through tough times, it was clearly an important factor in my recovery and finally my rehabilitation back into a normal life. What I have also learnt about love is that I can only be intimate to the degree that I am willing to be open and vulnerable. This not only applies to intimacy with Penny but also with my family and friends. I have discovered by my openness and at times vulnerability that this has enabled others to be open back to me. This results in amazing growth in relationships. They are suddenly much deeper and much more meaningful. Clearly these matters were very important to my wellbeing. I will let David Suzuki have the final word on this matter:

> *As each of us develops, we need companions to define and extend our sense of self, and a community in which we find opportunities for a mate, for rewarding activity and for conviviality. These needs are absolute, inalienable, and where they are not met we suffer, even perish.*

On a related subject I want to mention the impact that touch had on me while I was dealing with my illness. I have mentioned elsewhere that my friends and family visited me regularly and I was physically touched frequently. Although I was raised in a family where I received lots of hugs I didn't understand the impact that being touched, especially being hugged can have on wellbeing until my illness. I became the recipient of many warm friendly caring hugs. Touching is a form of intimacy and as I commented above intimacy is important in healing. I understand there is much written about the therapeutic value of touch and being hugged. From my personal experience I have no doubt that they are therapeutic. By the way I was held and touched I knew that there was deep care and concern for me. It's interesting that this has freed me to touch in return. I am now able to greet many of my male and female friends with a warm embrace when we meet. I am less self-conscious about hugging. This has been a wonderful and further way of deepening my friendships. In her book *The Joy of Touching*, Helen Colton explains that the haemoglobin in the blood increases significantly when we are hugged and touched. Hence it would seem that hugging and touching could be wonderful in assisting us to stay healthy.

It's interesting the thoughts that come when you have plenty of time and not a lot of capacity to entertain yourself. One of the thoughts that came to me about my health after I had been in hospital for some time was in relation to the attention I was getting because I was ill. I had so many visitors, lots of cards and messages and was the focus of attention by doctors and nurses. The thought crept in that if I recovered this would stop. I then remembered that I had read about people choosing to be ill because of the attention they received, which apparently can happen with people who feel that this is the only way they can get attention. I understand that this is also behaviour we learn as children (parents fuss over us when we are ill) and then this may become unconscious behaviour in adulthood. I quickly dismissed the thoughts and decided that while the attention was wonderful I was planning to get well as quickly as possible. Clearly I needed to be well to be able to run.

I reported earlier in this book departing hospital at one point in the process weighing a little over 50 kilograms and being unable to walk without assistance. The road back from there was tough. My legs didn't work properly, I found eating difficult and the smallest amount of activity exhausted me. However, I had during my time in hospital decided that running was a very important part of my life and that I would do the hard work necessary to get back to the point where I could run again. It was indeed hard work and at times frustrating because of the slow progress and discomfort. I felt that as running was an important and integral part of my healthy life I would not be fully recovered until I could run again. I had learnt early in my running career that running provided much more than physical wellbeing and having cancer reinforced to me the importance of the mental or psychological aspects of running. I had missed that overall sense of peace that I derived from running. My healing would somehow be incomplete without the inner wellbeing that came from running. As Deepak Chopra put it:

> *Health is not just the absence of disease. It's an inner joyfulness that should be ours all the time – a state of positive well-being.*

I had discovered that for me running contributed significantly to this inner joyfulness and this state of positive wellbeing. Hence I wasn't yet ready to discard my running shoes.

I have taken lots of time to think about what happened to me and what impact this has had on me as a person. I have thought about the question of what has been the key change or learning for me. My conclusion is that accepting and welcoming change is vital to me, my journey as a person and to my personal growth. Facing many difficult situations provided me with opportunities to change and grow. I found the words of David Schnarch (*Passionate Marriage*) to be very useful in facing difficulties and making change (he calls the difficulties gridlocks or problems). Facing one of these difficulties he says is like climbing a mountain:

... rather than trying to control the terrain and weather, you can relax and enjoy the climb. When you're tense and feeling out of control, the climb seems more difficult. It helps if you keep in mind that you never really master the mountain – you master yourself in the process of climbing the mountain. The mountain remains the same it is you who has changed.

There were many times in hospital when I thought about changing the terrain and weather, but after self-talk I usually came back to making change in how I thought about what was happening. Schnarch goes on to say that we have to face several mountains before we feel confident in ourselves and that we can't wait until we feel safe and secure before we take the risk to make changes. Understanding the importance of change and how I deal with it has been a very important outcome for me from having a major health problem.

Because I had cancer I have made progress with my personal growth. I have had some things confirmed, I have certainly had some new learnings, my understanding of some things has deepened and I feel as though I have gained a number of new insights. These things may not have happened without cancer coming along and forcing me to confront myself in different and challenging ways.

I have read about some people who have looked back on an illness and commented that they were glad they had the illness because it changed their life. I can't quite do that, as there were lots of experiences associated with my illness that I would rather have avoided. However I can acknowledge that having cancer has changed me in some very positive ways. It's raised for me lots of questions, which I am still exploring. I am sure I will find some more answers but I am equally sure that this will prompt more questions and so the quest goes on. Each new insight takes me a little bit closer to the person that I truly am; the real me.

Am I a better person as a result of having cancer? Am I a softer or harder person? I think I am a little wiser, better able to understand myself and better equipped to continue to grow as a person. I think I am a little softer because I am less judgemental and more ready to deal with and experience feelings rather than thoughts. However, it can be difficult to see yourself in a completely unbiased way and hence my family and friends may have a different perspective to mine. Clearly I have a lot of things to continue to work on, including staying healthy.

I will leave this chapter with some further words from Deepak Chopra:

> *The cause of disease is often extremely complex, but one thing can be said for certain: no one has proved that getting sick is necessary.*

Chapter 10

Life After Cancer

For oft, when on my couch I lie
In vacant or in pensive mood,
They flash upon that inward eye
Which is the bliss of solitude;
And then my heart with pleasure fills,
And dances with the daffodils.

Daffodils. William Wordsworth

I feel as though I have been on a remarkable journey that has involved lots of twists and turns, clearly some learnings and personal growth for me and I am now left with a healthy body and I think a reasonably healthy enquiring mind. Life is great and I am truly able to dance with the daffodils.

I have adjusted to life with a stoma. One of the many doctors that I had while in hospital said to me soon after I acquired the stoma that the only difference from now on would be that I would do all my toileting standing up. This was a true statement in part, but life with a stoma involves a little more than standing up when using the toilet. I initially had teething problems with the stoma, which included some difficulties with rashes and itchy skin but they were rectified relatively easily. For example it was just a matter of changing appliances until I found the one compatible with my skin. The prolapsing was a major difficulty but that was rectified with surgery. It now works very well for me and doesn't prevent me from doing any of the things I enjoy, such as running and travelling.

Penny and I have travelled to Asia, North and South America, North West Africa, Central America and Europe without any problems. My suitcase is of course now partly filled with replacement bags, plates and wipes. However, I have developed a routine around this including working out how much to take. It could clearly be a disaster if I miscalculated the number I needed.

My stoma does have a 'mind' of its own (if indeed stomas have a mind) and often emits loud noises, which are largely beyond my control. This seems to happen at times when I am in a place with people and there is period of silence. It can be a little embarrassing. My friends are aware of this and ignore it. I was involved in a court case as part of my role as president of a large running organisation and had to meet with our solicitor and barrister to discuss possible options. We sat in a very quiet conference room and the barrister outlined a proposed strategy and then looked at me to respond. At that very point my stoma made a very loud and prolonged noise. I felt extremely embarrassed and tried to cover by saying that ever since surgery my 'system' sometimes made unexpected noises (they were not aware that I had cancer, surgery and a stoma). The barrister looked at me and said: 'Oh I thought that was your mobile phone'. I later thought that I was sure that I would not want that ring tone on my mobile phone (even though it would be unique).

A ritual that I now participate in each month is to visit the local stoma association to collect my monthly supplies. The scheme, funded by the federal government and operated by local non-government associations, is great. It provides all the appliances and associated gear to people like me free of charge. The smooth running of the scheme takes place through the voluntary work of association members. Stoma nurses are also available to assist with advice and support. The person who manages my association office (Lindsay until very recently) and helpers do a wonderful job for which I am grateful. My only cost is to pay a small annual membership fee to belong to the association.

After my last time in hospital I have had ongoing consultations with my surgeon and oncologist. I always preceded these visits with a blood test and sometimes a CT scan. I have also had two more colonoscopies. All tests have been normal and the doctors have been very pleased with the results and my progress. I recently had my five-year consultation with both the surgeon and oncologist. Given the state of my health I no longer need to see these doctors. I felt a strange sensation when I walked out of their consulting rooms for the last time. I was pleased but it was a bit like saying goodbye to long-time friends. However it was wonderful to have the five-year clearance. There is no sign of cancer. I intend to keep it that way. My general health is great. My only requirement now is to be sure to have a colonoscopy every three years.

I have retired from work. This was a decision I made when I had a two-month period in hospital and when there were many health problems, complications and setbacks. I decided that although I had always enjoyed work I had other things that I wanted to do in my life and I wanted to get on with them. These other things include writing, reading, music, travel, cooking, movies, time with family and friends, photography and, of course, running. It's been good to have time to do all of them and to look forward to doing them all over and over again. My only difficulty is to try and fit into each day the things that I want to do. What a wonderful challenge to be faced with each day.

I have been working on two manuscripts for several years on the subject of emigration to the Australian colonies in small sailing vessels during the nineteenth century. These old sailing vessels and the people who emigrated in them have been a long-term interest and passion of mine. The spirit and determination of these nineteenth century pioneers has always fascinated and inspired me. I have at last had some time to do some real work on my manuscripts and managed to complete one and have it published. This was a great sense of achievement for me. The book tells the story of some 260 men, women and children who emigrated from England to the colony of Adelaide in 1850 on board the vessel *Stag*. (See: *The Stag Diary – Passage to Colonial Adelaide 1850*). I have recently completed a second and much larger manuscript (*Farewell to Old England Forever*) and it has now been published.

I started this book with a discussion about running and so it's appropriate that I finish it that way too. My fears at the start of this journey included thoughts that I might not be able to run again. I can report that running is again an integral part of my daily activity. I have adjusted to running with a stoma (only causing me an occasional problem on very hot days when the excess moisture sometimes affects the adhesive on the plate). I am back to running each morning before breakfast – usually between about 8 and 10 kilometres. I have participated in some club events and completed a half marathon (21.1 km) in a time of a little over 1 hour 50 minutes (not as good as my 90-minute times just before my illness, but a time I was pleased with). Spending a couple of months preparing for that event was a bit of a physical and mental challenge. However I was able to prove to myself that I could still do long training runs at around the 20-kilometre distance. I am also supporting my local running club by helping with events.

About six months after my five-year clearance by my doctors the question arose as to the possibility of another marathon. Some of my running mates had been saying for a while that it must be time for me to consider doing one more. It was jokingly said that I would not have fully recovered until I demonstrated that I could do another marathon. I had also some encouragement from Penny to think about it. I think she knew how important marathon running had been to me and that completing another one would truly mark my complete recovery. There was no pressure but rather support and encouragement to think seriously about it. In my mind I was healthy and the doctors had said I no longer had cancer. I was running every day and was reasonably fit. However my times were slow compared to pre-illness times, I did not breath as efficiently, I had difficulty running up hills (not like my last marathon hill training), I took longer to recover and I was several years older. I could remember back almost six years to training for my last marathon and recalled how demanding the training was week after week for about three months. The question I asked myself was whether I would be able to cope with that level of training and sustain it for three months. I had written a marathon-training guide for those wishing to run their first marathon – would I be able to follow the type of marathon training program I had recommended to other runners?

I decided that I wanted to find out and so began a period of building up my overall distances in order to have a good enough base from which to build a three-month marathon-training program.

I steadily built up the base over a two-month period and was then ready for the real marathon training. My goal was simple. I had to increase my long weekly run each week so that I fairly quickly reached a distance of 35 kilometres. I wanted to have five or six runs at around that distance before the marathon. These longer runs weren't easy. In fact I had forgotten just how hard they could be. My first run of 20 kilometres was hard and I still had to add another 15 kilometres to that in order to be able to do several runs of around 35 kilometres. Each week I added a few kilometres and by the end of the first month I had reached 30 kilometres. Three weeks later I was up to the 35-kilometre mark. I managed to fit four of these in followed by two 36-kilometre runs prior to the marathon. They were all hard work. My legs were tired, sore and at time painful in the last five or so kilometres of each of these long runs.

I had to remind myself that this was the nature of marathon training. I was training my body physically and mentally to be able to run the 42.2 kilometres of a marathon. I also needed to remind myself that it would hurt in the last 10 kilometres of the marathon and I had to be mentally tough enough to run through it.

I completed a couple of the long runs feeling very light-headed and was forced to lie down. The long runs did improve but I was still very tired after each one and my body was taking longer to recover. Not only had I been through significant health problems but I was now six years older and in my 70th year. I decided to have a rest and recovery day after each long run. This was new for me as I had in the past always gone for a run on the day after a long run. However it was now necessary to add a rest day to my program and it helped enormously.

After all those weeks of aching and tired legs it was eventually marathon day. Malcolm, a close friend of mine, had said during my recovery if I ever ran another marathon he would run his first marathon with me. Malcolm had made this statement as a way of encouraging and supporting me in my recovery, a wonderful act of friendship. On the cool autumn morning of the marathon Malcolm lined up with me feeling rather nervous and wondering what on earth he had committed himself to. While we waited for the start I had lots of friends offering words of encouragement. We were soon underway on our 42.2-kilometre journey. I received an enormous amount of support along the way. I had a fellow runner ask me: 'Are you Dougie?'. When I replied yes he said that clearly I had an incredible number of friends.

And so Malcolm and Dougie finished and in respectable times, both experiencing aching and dead legs in the last few kilometres as you do in a marathon. I was just aiming for a finish without walking but was delighted to finish in 4 hours 2 minutes, with (young) Malcolm about 5 minutes quicker. When I crossed the line I was quickly embraced by a friend, Sarah, who is an elite athlete and one-time World Ironman Champion, with the statement that I was an inspiration. Another marathoner friend, PK, also embraced me and told me that I was a legend. While it was wonderful to be described as inspirational and a legend I was just pleased to have been able to finish. This one was important and special. It was an incredible feeling of elation finishing another marathon and having so much support. I felt a few tears trickle down my face and for the next week I floated on a mental high. Although I had previously completed 21 marathons this one was different. I now knew that it was still possible for me to again run a marathon. I had now recovered from cancer.

Malcolm (right) and Dougie a few minutes after finishing

A short time after the marathon Penny and I were attending an annual runners lunch, which was largely a social occasion enabling runners to spend time together, have fun, enjoy good food and a few glasses of wine. The event always involved two presentations. One award was a humorous one and the other was presented in recognition of a special running achievement by one of the group, such as a setting a new record. These presentations were made and then it was announced that a special presentation would be made to a runner who had been an outstanding example of persistence, achievement and an inspiration to the running community. After what seemed like a long build up my name was announced and I then received a standing ovation. This was an incredible surprise and I was momentarily unable to move. I felt very emotional, very humble and had difficulty holding back tears. My running friends saw my journey back from cancer and my determination to get back to normal life, including back to running, culminating with the marathon as very special. I find it difficult to think of myself as inspirational. I was simply focussed on doing what I had always done: enjoying life, enjoying friends and of course running. What a special bunch of people these runners are.

In a moment of euphoria in the week after the marathon I wondered if I might be able to back up with a second marathon in about three months. This was something that I had never attempted before – on three different occasions in the past I had done two marathons in a year, but in each case those marathons were at least six months apart. Feeling so incredibly buoyed by my recent achievement I reasoned that if I could recover fully during the next month my level of marathon fitness might enable me get back into marathon training mode and complete a sufficient number of long runs to be able to do another marathon in about three months. I had in mind a north coast event that I had never participated in previously. It was a big event with a relatively flat course but would be much warmer than my home town (by now well into autumn and cooling as a result of early snow falls in the nearby mountains). I disclosed my thinking to Penny who was a little surprised but as usual very supportive.

After 10 days of no running followed by about another 10 days of very light running I began to pick up the distance again with a focus on the weekly long run. My first post-marathon longer run was 20 kilometres, which I felt was long enough to determine if I had recovered from the marathon. It went fairly well with only some minor protests from my legs. The next week I did 25 kilometres, then 28 kilometres and the following week 33 kilometres. I now felt back on track but would need to do at least three runs longer than 33 kilometres before the event to be ready. Fitting the long runs in to my schedule proved to be a challenge because we had to travel several times for family reasons during this time. However I did manage to fit in two runs at 35 kilometres and two at 36 kilometres and a run of 17 kilometres during the two-week taper period just prior to the event. These long runs are always a challenge but they all went well except for the first of the 36-kilometre runs, which was extremely difficult and left me feeling sore and tired. I felt that I had done enough work to be able to complete another marathon.

We flew north for the event from a cold frosty winter morning to sunshine with very mild winter temperatures. After a day and a half to adjust I rose at 4.30 am on marathon morning to have breakfast. This would be my last opportunity to carbohydrate-load before the start of the marathon at 7.20 am. Special buses took runners, including me, to the start area. The early morning temperature was cool but the forecast was for a maximum of 22 degrees Celsius. There was only sparse cloud cover and so it would quickly warm up. The start time arrived, the gun was fired and about 6,000 runners set off to conquer the 42.2-kilometre course. Many of the runners had signalled at the start that this was their first attempt at a marathon. I decided that despite the forecast temperature I would stick with my normal marathon strategy and run as fast as my training would permit at an even pace (hoping that the temperature would not interfere with this plan).

This strategy worked and I had a good run finishing strongly over the last 10 kilometres and as a result passed many runners who were clearly finding those last few kilometres very difficult. Perhaps they were some of the first timers who hadn't prepared sufficiently or who had run too fast in the early part of the event. It's so easy in marathon running to get carried away in the first part of the event and then pay dearly in the final 10 or so kilometres when your system shuts down, you hit the wall and can barely walk. I was surprised to pass so many runners who were either running very slowly or walking. After 42 kilometres I turned into the finish shute for the last 200 metres and managed to increase my pace for a strong finish. I felt good afterwards, Penny was very excited and I was extremely pleased. I didn't feel as emotional as I had when I finished the previous event but I nevertheless felt a great sense of achievement. My time was good and even though I had been conscious of the temperature I don't think it had an impact on my performance. The event was over and so I had managed to run two marathons just under three months apart. Penny is sure that I will now keep running marathons until the wheels fall off. We will see, but clearly the passion for distance running is still there.

It wasn't long before I was planning what my marathon goals might be in the following year[2].

I have always been an optimistic person and have for a long time believed that anything is possible. I now know that to be true.

Although my days of fast running are over I am so pleased that my health problems haven't prevented me from putting the shoes on and going for a run. I am much slower now and I regret this and at times I recall some of my fast times and triumphs (which my running friends delight in doubting). This seems to be something us runners do when we get together. I have mentioned previously that runners enjoy fun and socialising and often this leads to reminiscing and singing. In fact when singing together we always include a song entitled the *Runner's Lament* (the words of which were composed by close friend Richard, see Appendix I). That song is always sung with real feeling and it laments that we don't run like we used to. The last verse particularly captures that shared feeling (sung to the tune of Leonard Cohen's *Hallelujah*):

Maybe there's a God above
With those who run they share a love
Moments to be felt and treasured with you

---

[2] Since writing this book the author has completed a further two marathons.

So if times are slow, we don't care
The running soul is what we share
Don't mind if we can't run just like we used to.
Like we used to, like we used to.
Like we used to, like we used to.

Well it feels like the story has come full circle, starting with running and a marathon (and a cancer) and finishing with running and a marathon or two (and no cancer).

That after marathon glow of success.

To finish a final word from Leunig:

Let it go. Let it out.
Let it all unravel.
Let it free and it can be.
A path on which to travel.

Appendix I

The Runners Lament ©
Words by Richard Faulks

I heard there was a running race
If I trained hard, I'd have the pace
But you don't really care for such pain, do you.
It goes like this,
The nerves, the gun,
The lactic legs, the burning lungs
But baffled coach says, 'you don't run like you used to'
Like you used to, like you used to,
Like you used to, like you used to.

Your faith was strong, but you needed more,
Your smelly shoes sat by the door
The entries in past diaries did inspire you.
So you tried again up Heartbreak Hill,
Your knee gave out,
You had a spill,
And from your lips, 'I can't run like I used to'
Like I used to, like I used to,
Like I used to, like I used to.

We all said we've been here before,
The Lane Cove Half we've forgotten more
I'm sure I had less pain before I knew you
I've seen the frosts on the winter morns,
The tightened calves, the hamstrings torn,
When I wake up, I don't walk like I used to.
Like I used to, like I used to,
Like I used to, like I used to.

There was a time when I felt quite sane
Then Pat's only words were 'forget the pain'
And all I wanted was to go run with you
We did the hills, the Triple Tri,
That 42 ks sure made me cry
My heart is strong, but legs not like they used to.
Like they used to, like they used to.
Like they used to, like they used to.

Maybe there's a God above
With those who run they share a love
Moments to be felt and treasured with you
So if times are slow, we don't care
The running soul is what we share
Don't mind if we can't run just like we used to.
Like we used to, like we used to.
Like we used to, like we used to.

Note: The above song is sung to the tune of Leonard Cohen's *Hallelujah*. Richard Faulks has written a number of running songs.

Annotated References and Some Useful Reading

In writing this book I have referred on a number of occasions to authors whose writings I have found insightful, challenging and sometimes controversial during my quest for greater personal understanding and growth. I found many of their books helpful and affirming during my illness and recovery. I had read most of these books prior to my cancer diagnosis but found that I returned to reread some of them or parts of them many times after the diagnosis. The following list contains those that have been significant in my own growth, recovery and in my rehabilitation process. I have annotated each reference in order that the reader might understand why these publications were useful to me in my personal journey and so that these publications may be potentially useful to readers.

Armstrong, Lance. *It's Not About the Bike.* Allen & Unwin 2000.

> (His approach to dealing with cancer was helpful to me in the early stages of treatment, particularly when I started chemotherapy. More recent revelations about his drug taking have severely damaged his reputation and the sport of cycling).

Bach, Richard. *Jonathan Livingston Seagull, a Story*. Pan Books Ltd, London 1973.

(This is a fable in novella form about a seagull learning about life and flight, and a homily about self-perfection. Contains some interesting insights and lessons.)

Boynton, Sandra. *Consider Love, Its Moods and Many Ways*. Simon & Schuster 2002.

(This book deals with love in a simplistic, sentimental and soulful way but has some profound illustrations and contains many curious modes of love and it rhymes.)

Bryant, John. *3:59.4 The Quest to Break the 4 Minute Mile*. Arrow Books 2005.

(This is the story of the quest that lasted over 70 years of those runners who raced to conquer the 4-minute mile. I found it inspirational because of the extraordinary courage, dedication and determination that was shown by many runners in their endeavour to break the 4-minute mile).

Carlson, Richard. *Don't Sweat the Small Stuff*. Bantam 1997.

(This an easy to read guide on how to avoid stress and live in the now.)

Chopra, Deepak. *Ageless Body Timeless Mind*. Rider 2008.

(A wonderful book in which Chopra challenges the reader by asserting ageing is much more of a choice than we think. He asserts that sickness and ageing are created by our gaps in self-knowledge.)

Chopra, Deepak. *Journey into Healing. Awakening the Wisdom within You*. Rider 1994.

(In this book Chopra has listed his essential ideas to create an experience – a journey into healing.)

Chopra, Deepak. *Reinventing the Body, Resurrecting the Soul*. Rider 2009.

(This work follows closely what was contained in *Ageless Body Timeless Mind*. Here Chopra examines the profound connection between our thoughts and our health and shows how we can break through our past conditioning to reinvent our bodies, reconnect with our souls and enjoy lives that are rich in joy and meaning.)

Chopra, Deepak. *Synchro Destiny*. Rider 2003.

(In this book Chopra explains that coincidences are messages about the miraculous potential of each moment and how if we understand the forces that shape them we can transform our lives.)

Colton, Helen. *The Joy of Touching*. Seaview/Putnam 1983.

(This book explores the importance and power of touching.)

Emoto, Masaru. *The Hidden Messages in Water*. Atria Books 2001.

(This is a fascinating work by a Japanese scientist in exploring how the molecules in water are affected by our thoughts, words and feelings. As humans and the earth are composed mostly of water his message is one of personal health, global environmental renewal and a practical plan for peace that starts with each of us.)

Emoto, Masaru. *The True Power of Water, Healing and Discovering Ourselves.* Atria Books 2005.

(This book expands on Emoto's earlier work by examining how energy is transmitted through water and how through our interaction with water we can send ripples of love and gratitude, the most powerful of all emotions, to every person on the planet.)

Fixx, Jim. *The Complete Book of Running.* Random House 1977.

(This is the classic book on running which had a profound impact on transforming running from something that elite athletes did to a mass participation activity. It was also very influential in promoting the marathon, an endurance event, which subsequently became possible for all runners to conquer.)

Griffiths, Andy. *The Day My Bum Went Psycho.* Pan Macmillan Australia, 2001.

(This is a typical of Andy Griffiths book – a bit of fun and easy reading. It is the story of Zack, the main character, on his journey, involving courage and endurance and confrontation with some of the 'biggest, ugliest and meanest' bums ever to roam the face of the earth.)

Haggar, Fatima A & Boushey, Robin P. *Colorectal Cancer Epidemiology: Incidence, Mortality, Survival and Risk Factors.*

(This is a paper that brings together research findings and data on colorectal cancer.)

Hay, Louise L. *You Can Heal Your Life*. Hay House Australia Pty Ltd 2006.

(This is probably the best known of Louise Hay's work. It explores how if we are willing to do the mental work then almost anything can be healed. She explains how limiting our beliefs and ideas are often the cause of illness and then demonstrates how we can change our thinking and improve the quality of our lives.)

Horner, Karen. *Neurosis and Human Growth*. W.W.Norton & Company Inc, 1970.

(Horner discusses the neurotic process as a special form of human development, the antithesis of healthy growth. The book includes an analysis of the forces that work for and against our realisation of our potential.)

Lama, Dalai. *The Essence of Happiness*. Hodder 2001.

(In this book the Dalai Lama offers simple advice on how to defeat day-to-day depression, anxiety, anger, jealousy and the myriad of emotions that get in the way of happiness.)

Leunig, Michael. *The Prayer Tree*. Collins Dove 1991.

(One of Leunig's books offering through poetry wisdom of the inner life drawn from reflection on the mystery of everyday life. The prayers address issues that affect everyone: changing seasons, love, relationships, dark times.)

Mackay, Hugh. *The Art of Belonging. It's Not Where You Live, It's How You Live.* Pan Macmillan, 2014.

(In the *Art of Belonging* Mackay advances the argument put forward in *The Good Life*: a 'good life' is not lived in isolation or in the pursuit of independent goals; a good life is lived at the heart of a thriving community, among people we trust, and within an environment of mutual respect. He reveals the beautiful symmetry of the human condition: we need communities, but communities also need us. He argues that we should take responsibility for the places where we live by engaging, volunteering, joining up and joining in.)

Mackay, Hugh. *The Good Life. What makes a Life Worth Living?* Pan Macmillan Australia, 2013.

(In this book Mackay asks and answers the ultimate question: What makes a life worth living? His conclusion, drawn from his many years of research, is provocative and passionately argued. A good life is not measured by security, wealth, status, achievement or levels of happiness. A good life is determined by our capacity for selflessness and our willingness to connect with those around us in a meaningful and useful way.)

Matthews, Andrew. *Being Happy!* Media Masters Pty Ltd 1995.

(This book is about balance in relationships, finding career success, prosperity and peace of mind. It deals with what to do when things get tough, self talk, the laws of life, enjoying your work, making more money, relationships, our mind as a magnet and focusing on what we want.)

Matthews, Andrew. *Follow Your Heart*. Seashell Publishers 1997.

(Like Matthews' other books this is easy to read and full of good tips and insights about love, peace of mind, dealing with disasters, bills, setbacks and not blaming others.)

Matthews, Andrew. *Making Friends*. Media Masters Pty Ltd 1997.

(This is a sequel to *Being Happy* and written in the same easy reading style. Its about what you must do if you want friendships, including enjoying people, being able to say no, rising above pettiness and dealing with prophets of doom.)

Murakami, Haruki. *What I Talk About When I Talk About Running*. Vintage 2009.

(This is Murakami's story of deciding to get fit and take up running. It's a memoir that is equal part travelogue, training log and reminiscences. He reflects on what part sport has had on his life and writing.)

Murphy, Joseph. *Secrets of the I Ching*. Parker Publishing Company Inc 1973.

(This book provides a down-to-earth practical way of understanding and using the wisdom contained in the 5,000 year old I Ching to provide you with guidance to undertake every day decisions: financial, romantic, social, personal.)

Ornish, Dean. *Love and Survival*. Random House Australia 1999.

(Ornish looks at the scientific basis for the healing power of intimacy. He identifies love and intimacy as the most powerful healing force that exists. The book has lots of insights and practical wisdom about protecting health and enhancing wellness.)

Runners World. Sole Motive Pty Ltd (published monthly).

(A great monthly magazine that has lots of stories about people who have overcome adversity, tips on improving running, achieving goals, scientific findings on health, fitness and wellbeing, guidance about healthy eating including recipes and of course information about events to enter and the latest running gear.)

Schnarch, David. *Passionate Marriage*. Scribe Publications 2000.

(A wonderful book about love and intimacy in a committed relationship. It includes an important discussion about the importance of differentiation in a relationship – the balancing of two basic life forces: the drive for individuality and the drive for togetherness. Achieving this balance is essential to a loving and intimate relationship.)

Suzuki, David. *The Sacred Balance*. Allen & Unwin 1997.

(David Suzuki discusses our relationship with the earth and how as creatures of the earth we are utterly dependent on its gifts of air, water, soil and the energy of the sun. He contends that as social animals we have an absolute need for love. He concludes that we have spiritual needs, which are ultimately rooted in nature, the source of our inspiration and belonging.)

Tolle, Eckhart. *A New Earth*. Penguin Group (Australia) 2005.

(In this book Tolle shatters modern ideas of ego and entitlement, self and society. He then sets out a path that leads to health and happiness.)

Tolle, Eckhart. *The Power of Now*. Hachette Australia 2004.

(This is a powerful book that challenges us to leave our analytical mind and the false sense of self it creates in order to become connected to the essence of our Being by living in the now. The book is a guide to spiritual enlightenment.)

Wheatley, Margaret J. *Leadership and the New Science. Disorder in a Chaotic World*. Berrett-Koehler Publishers, 1999.

(Wheatley talks about how we live in a time of chaos, which is rich in potential for new possibilities. She contends that we need new ideas, new ways of seeing and new relationships to help us now. In examining this she looks at the 'New Science' (discoveries in biology, chaos theory and quantum physics) and how they are changing our understanding of how the world works and provides guidance.)

Wilber, Ken. *The Simple Feeling Of Being, Embracing Your True Nature*. Shambhala 2004.

(Ken Wilber writes as a philosopher and psychologist and also from a background in Eastern spirituality and Western science. This book is a collection of inspirational mystical and instructional passages drawn from his many publications. They include contemplative poetry, commentary on the spiritual contributions of a number of well-known thinkers past and present, anecdotes of personal experience and practical spiritual instructions and guided meditation.)

Printed in the United States
By Bookmasters